R.J. Stewart
Biography

R.J. Stewart is a Scottish author, composer and musician living in the USA, wherein he was admitted in 1997 as a "Resident Alien of Extraordinary Ability," a category awarded to those with the highest achievements in the arts or sciences.

He has 41 books in publication worldwide, translated into many languages, and has recorded a wide range of music and meditational CDs, plus music for film, television, and theater productions in Britain, Canada, and the USA.

He teaches workshops and classes worldwide, has appeared in numerous films and documentaries, and gives concerts of his original music and songs, featuring the unique 80-stringed concert Psaltery and other instruments.

In 1988 R.J. Stewart founded the *Inner Temple Traditions InnerConvocation*™® program, which consists of a series of ongoing classes, publications, groups, and trained teachers working with spiritual and imaginative themes.

For further information, please visit the Stewart websites:

www.dreampower.com
www.rjstewart.org
www.rjstewart.net
www.innerconvocation.com

R.J. Stewart Books
P.O. Box 7803
Roanoke, VA 24019
www.rjstewart.net

ROBERT KIRK:

WALKER BETWEEN
THE WORLDS

• • •

A New Edition of
The Secret Commonwealth
of Elves, Fauns & Fairies

BY

R.J. STEWART

R.J. Stewart
Books

CONTENTS

The Jackman's Song, by Ben Jonson   vi
Acknowledgments   vii
Foreword by Jennifer Westwood   viii
Preface   xi
Introduction   1

THE SECRET COMMONWEALTH   19
Robert Kirk's Text (in Modern English)   21

Commentary on Aspects of the Text   72

APPENDICES
1. *The Rosicrucian Movement*, extract from an Essay by
   Thomas De Quincey   122
2. *The Lyke Wake Dirge*   124
3. *Tam Lin* (with commentary)   126
4. *Thomas Rhymer* (with commentary)   138
5. Prayers Spells and Charms from Devon and Scotland   153
6. Brigit, The Fire Goddess   158
7. The *Vita Merlini* Cosmology   161
8. Robert Kirk's Glossary   165
9. *Angels and Fairies*, extract from Harold Bailey's
   Archaic England   171

Bibliography   172
Index   175

In memory of Deirdre Green
who crossed into the
world of light March 1990

THE JACKMAN'S SONG

BY BEN JONSON

The Faiery beame upon you,
The starres to glister on you;
A Moone of light
In the Noone of night,
Till the fire-Drake hath o're-gone you.
The Wheele of fortune guide you,
The Boy with the Bow beside you,
Runne aye in the Way,
Till the Bird of day,
And the luckyer lot betide you.

ACKNOWLEDGEMENTS

This new edition of *The Secret Commonwealth* comes many years after I first read, in childhood, the incomplete edition prepared by Andrew Lang and published in the last century.[*4] In the intervening period a modern academic edition, edited by Stewart Sanderson, was published by the Folklore Society (Mistletoe Series).[5] This important edition lists all known manuscript sources and published variants, and I am indebted to the author for much valuable information.

I must also acknowledge Dr Deirdre Green, who, in 1982 introduced me to Kirk's fairy hill and took me to visit Kirk's grave and his home region in Aberfoyle, thus reawakening my dormant interest in *The Secret Commonwealth* and the lore of the Second Sight which runs in my own family. The concept of rendering the original text into modern English, in addition to a new short Commentary which I had long intended to write, was suggested to me by folklorist Jennifer Westwood during a bus journey through the Highlands of Scotland in pursuit of elusive ancient sites. In which situation, as Robert Kirk himself would say, such antic fancies as fairy-lore and wrestling with the wraiths and aery substance of his book were made sensible both to the intellectual and visive faculties.

R. J. STEWART
Bath, 1990

[*]Superior figures refer to items in the Bibliography.

FOREWORD

THE ROAD TO THE FAIRY KNOWE

The *Secret Commonwealth* of Robert Kirk (1644–97), minister of Aberfoyle, is one of the most important books about fairies ever written. It is quite the fullest account of the subject from the seventeenth century, a period when many country people in England as well as Scotland still believed implicitly in fairies, and antiquarians such as John Aubrey laboured to record their testimony.

Kirk and Aubrey recognised that in their day something valuable was fast being lost from the culture. Fairy belief had long been dying from natural causes – Chaucer as far back as the fourteenth century suggested that fairies were things of the past – but now the process was being accelerated by events. One was the seizure of political control by Protestant radicals under Cromwell's Commonwealth. Unlike the more tolerant Catholics before the Reformation, these extremists – Puritans, Presbyterians, and others – viewed things that smacked of paganism, including maypoles, fairies and Christmas, as idolatry, and suppressed them. It is no coincidence that, later, in Wales people said it was the Methodists who had driven out the fairies.

Another keynote of the seventeenth century was the foundation of the Royal Society (1662), which marked the official sanctioning of the new, emergent 'science'. The career of someone like Elias Ashmole (1617–92), antiquary, alchemist and astrologer (who left for posterity not only a spell for a catching a fairy but also the Ashmolean Museum, Oxford) would thereafter be impossible. While traditions of fairy thefts, fairy food, elf-shot, fairy ointment, changelings and the like remained current in England, Wales and Lowland Scotland down to the nineteenth century, actual belief in fairies and the related Second Sight survived latest among the Gaelic-speaking Highlanders of Scotland because they lived in the most inaccessible part of Britain, further out of the reach of authority and more remote from 'civilizing' influences – including the English language – than the rest of the population.

Kirk had an unparalleled opportunity to study their lore. A Gaelic speaker, he was minister of Balquidder for twenty-one years, before being called as minister to Aberfoyle, his birthplace, as successor to his father. His unique position in the community – as pastor and as his father's son – undoubtedly meant that sources of information were open to him that would have been closed to a mere passing antiquarian. But was Kirk indiscreet in telling the world what he knew? The people of Aberfoyle evidently thought so, for he had broken the age-old taboo of secrecy imposed by the fairies on those who witnessed their doings. When his body at length was found beside the Fairy Knowe (or hill) in Aberfoyle, traditionally a fairy dwelling, the rumour went round that it was only a 'stock', a simulacrum left by the fairies, and that Kirk himself had been taken to live under the Fairy Knowe.

This was a punishment from which he could be redeemed. According to a minister of Aberfoyle writing in 1806 (you will find the story in the pages that follow), his chance for redemption came shortly after the funeral, and was missed. Much later on, during the Second World War, an officer's wife who was renting the Manse at Aberfoyle and expecting a baby, was told that if the christening were held there, and during it a dirk was stuck in what was purported to be Kirk's chair, Kirk would be freed. Unfortunately, this seems not to have been tried and so Kirk still remains under the hill!

Kirk writes his account of the fairies in the flexible and

distinctive prose of the seventeenth century – a prose increasingly difficult for the general reader to comprehend. Moreover, the fullest text of Kirk's work, edited by Stewart Sanderson and published by the Folklore Society (1976), is uncompromisingly scholarly. Hopefully, this version, which smooths out difficulties without losing the rhythms of Kirk's speech, will make him more accessible. The rest, I leave R.J. Stewart to (as Kirk would have put it) 'discover'. We have argued over Kirk the length of Scotland, and, with the encouragement of friends, will likely do so till Kirk, or for that matter King Arthur, returns. But we all wholeheartedly agree that Kirk's experience of that secret commonwealth of the Hidden People is one that must be shared with a new generation.

JENNIFER WESTWOOD
London, 1990

PREFACE

ROBERT KIRK

Robert Kirk was a seventeenth-century Scottish clergyman. His major literary work, now virtually forgotten, though of revolutionary importance in his own day, consisted of translating psalms into Gaelic, and supervising a Gaelic edition of the Bible. But he also collected the beliefs of his Gaelic-speaking parishioners, and argued that such beliefs were not idle superstition but were compatible with the basics of Christianity. His *Secret Commonwealth* has long been one of the major sources for fairy lore and the Second Sight, though Kirk wrote this short book not as a 'folklore' collection, but as a general survey of the relationship between seership, Second Sight, and multifold worlds or dimensions – a survey which he held to contain truth, enduring tradition, and fragments of ancient wisdom.

For the modern reader or student of magical traditions there are many clear connections to shamanism, pagan Celtic religion, and elements of American Indian tradition in Kirk's short book. There seems to be a close connection between many of the techniques of vision and magic, and the literal nature of otherworlds described in the seventeenth century by Robert Kirk, and the vastly popular twentieth-century works of Carlos Castaneda, who claims to be writing from an Indian tradition of sorcery. Whether or not we accept Castaneda as being fully derived from genuine American

Indian magical arts, there is no doubt that both Celtic and Indian traditions share a number of curious features. Perhaps the most fascinating and paradoxical is that of literal physical translation into other worlds, either deliberately or through synchronous patterns or 'accidents'. Robert Kirk was the first person to set many of these traditions out in writing, in an English language analysis, drawing from immediate personal experience with his parishioners in Scotland.

The few handwritten copies of the original book that were first circulated seem to have caused a stir. A copy of the book was probably read by no less a person than Samuel Pepys, who was at that time the spy-master for King Charles II, and very influential in the rebuilding of the Royal Navy and establishing new scientific research.[6] Pepys had already investigated, at some risk to himself, certain Spanish seers and sorcerers, who were renowned for seeing at a distance. It seems that the Second Sight, in Britain as well as Spain, was taken seriously enough to merit its assessment as a military weapon – modern studies along similar lines are now being carried out by both the USA and the USSR, and there has long been an unconfirmed rumour that Britain has a well-established 'esoteric' research group under governmental control. Whatever the true situation at present, such matters may be traced back to at least as early as Dr John Dee,[7] who was seer, astrologer and cryptographer for Queen Elizabeth I.

Kirk, however, was not remotely interested in militaristic applications, for he was a deeply religious and mystical man, and a hard-working, active clergyman devoted to the betterment of his flock. But there is a further element to Kirk, for in addition to recording fairy lore and Celtic belief, he undoubtedly lived through such belief himself. Kirk was a seventh son, such as were widely believed to be susceptible to magical and spiritual dimensions. Despite his important role as a churchman and literary figure, he became wrapped in the Otherworldly traditions.

Robert Kirk is said, to this day, to be entrapped in the Otherworld; in the Aberfoyle region of Scotland he is reckoned not to have died, but to have been translated into fairyland. It should be emphasised that the Celtic fairyland is not a realm of cosy little elves and sprites, but as Kirk describes it, an entire world with powerful beings living in it according to their own natural laws. We also know from early Irish tradition that the *sidh* or fairy people were the old gods and goddesses, and on a more primal level, were the Ancestors of the people of the Land. A curious tale is related of attempts to bring about Kirk's return, and the historical Kirk (now the Otherworld Kirk) is associated with a fairy hill which may still be visited.

Thus we have the paradoxical situation where an historical person becomes part of an enduring magical tradition. Kirk is perhaps the last known representative of those mysterious seers who vanished into other worlds: we may include the historical Thomas Rhymer (thirteenth century), the legendary Tam Lin, and the major figure of Merlin in this same tradition. The validity of Kirk as a priest and literary figure puts a new emphasis upon the power of tradition, which is so often represented in modern thought as being merely the survival of oddments from the past.

When we compare Kirk to other historical or semi-historical persons related to Otherworldly experiences, we find a co-herent and often systematic tradition. This tradition may, in itself, be traced back to primal roots, to cultures in which the relationship between humanity and the land are paramount. Yet within such a relationship is the seed of religion, metaphysics, philosophy, and complex systems of magical psychology. Such systems persisted in various forms from ancient times, and have reappeared from the Renaissance through to the present day. The modern popular interest in 'occult' matters is founded upon such traditions, though sometimes in a corrupt and trivialised form.

To examine Kirk we should not assume that we are dealing only with folklore in the sense of literary preservation or a collection of specimens of Gaelic superstitions: *we are dealing with a living person who experienced and attempted to formulate the knowledge of another world*. Kirk saw this world as being close to our own, and not in any way counter to religion or to rational thought. He argued from a metaphysical standpoint, but regarded his concepts as reaching right through into manifestation, into personal and collective experience. He frequently emphasised the presence of a fragmentary but coherent world-view held by both the Gaelic seers and the inhabitants of that Secret Commonwealth which they perceived. The reality of this Otherworld or dimension was accepted by the Celts, and indeed by Kirk himself.

A re-evaluation of Kirk, based upon his own comments and perceptions in addition to related individual items of folklore or belief, is long overdue. When we approach his work in this manner, we find it in keeping with the perennial mystical and magical/psychological traditions of the world. Furthermore it offers firm historical evidence that dates active traditions of Otherworld vision, magical techniques, and physical translation into normally unseen dimensions.

INTRODUCTION

The Secret Commonwealth is generally regarded as a classic text on Gaelic folklore; it was written in 1690 or possibly 1691 by Robert Kirk, a Scottish Episcopalian minister deeply interested and involved in the traditions of fairies and Second Sight that were widespread among his Gaelic-speaking parishioners. Consequently scholars studying such beliefs use Kirk's book as a prime source for comparison with more recent popular beliefs, as it is one of the earliest accounts of fairy lore in the English language.

Kirk was no mere ignorant country priest, but a learned scholar, linguist and writer, and, of equal importance in the present context, a man of spiritual conviction and intuition. His involvement with Second Sight, however, may run even deeper than all of the foregoing, for he was a seventh son, and such people are traditionally said to be born with certain inherent powers of Second Sight and of healing. Kirk discusses this tradition in several places in his text, and we shall return to it again. He does not, however, state directly that he had Second Sight, though there are some textual implications that he had the healing touch. It would hardly have been politic for a clergyman to declare publicly that he was a seer, though there is no doubt whatsoever that Kirk affirms the Second Sight and the existence of the Fairy Race, using all the scholarly logical and philosophical techniques, citations and arguments at his disposal to do so. And as we shall discover, he also argues that there is no contradiction between contact with the Secret

Commonwealth and its inhabitants, and the practice of good Christianity.

The collective traditions which Kirk discusses were extensively found: we need only turn to W.Y. Evans Wentz' lengthy study of *The Fairy Faith in Celtic Countries* written in the early twentieth century,[5] to find many examples from direct contact with Irish or Breton people, who could not possibly have read or even known of Kirk's book, which are either identical or very close to those cited and described by Kirk some 300 years before. The work of Evans Wentz appeared during a powerful literary poetic and academic revival of interest in Celtic tradition, which involved writers such as W.B.Yeats, George Russell (known as AE), and others of equal stature in creativity and scholarship.[1] More recently Dr Anne Ross, herself Gaelic-speaking, has published a short study, *The Folklore of the Scottish Highlands*[2] which includes contemporary examples of continuing tradition. Kirk himself correctly affirmed that the Second Sight and fairy contact were very ancient occurrences perpetuated into his own time among simple country people: modern folklore has shown how enduring such traditions are.

Apart from that of Kirk, a number of other seventeenth- and eighteenth-century accounts of the Second Sight exist, ranging from books to letters,[3] and the subject aroused much interest. Dr Johnson, the eminent rationalist and sceptic, compiler of one of the first definitive dictionaries of English, investigated Second Sight on his tour of the Hebrides. He recorded that it was so common that it could be acquired temporarily (usually by the technique carefully described by Kirk on page 33) in exchange for a bag of tea, which at that time was a great delicacy and rarity in the Highlands and Islands.

Andrew Lang, the great Scottish scholar and historian, published an incomplete and somewhat confusing edition of *The Secret Commonwealth* in 1893, based upon the earlier 1815 edition that had been, reputedly, edited by Sir Walter Scott.[5] Lang's introduction linked the text and traditions of Second Sight and fairy lore with the current fashion and enthusiasm among certain scholars and scientists for spiritualism and extrasensory perception, with which he was involved, including comparisons to experiments and reports being assembled by the Society for Psychical Research. The only modern and complete edition that reproduces Kirk's text as exactly as possible from early manuscripts, is, as mentioned [in our Preface], that edited by Stewart Sanderson for the Folklore Society[2], though there are a small number of incomplete or confused editions based on the nineteenth-century versions.[5]

Although researchers and experts from the nineteenth century onwards have regarded Second Sight and fairy lore as aspects of folk tradition, or in the case of Lang as an early source of psychic and spiritualist evidence, such attitudes were certainly not those taken by Kirk, or indeed by a number of his contemporaries. We shall examine Kirk's own comments and his underlying beliefs on the subject as we proceed, but the main interest in the Sight among his contemporaries was one that seems only too modern: it was investigated as a possible source of espionage.

In Lord Tarbett's letter to the distinguished scientist Robert Boyle, which is quoted and commented on by Kirk (pages 39–45) we find one of a number of such scientific-military investigations. In a letter from Lord Reay written in 1699 (some seven years after Kirk's death) to Samuel Pepys, the subject is mentioned. Lord Reay had a copy of *The Secret Commonwealth*, one of a small number of handwritten copies which had been circulated in London, initially to people whom Kirk had met during one of his visits as translator of the Bible into Gaelic.

In 1684 Pepys, a member of the Royal Society which investigated and promoted scientific advances, of which Boyle was also a member, had travelled to Spain. Among other activities, he made a thorough investigation of the *saludadors* of Seville. These were seers who had a widespread reputation of being able to prophecy, perform cures, and see at a distance. He also investigated the *mal de ojo* or evil eye, and concluded and reported that it was all fraud.[7] It seems likely that Pepys' interest in the seers was in the context of his powerful role in rebuilding the Royal Navy – did the Spaniards have people who could spy upon the English at a distance? It also seems likely that his interest in Kirk's book was based upon a similar curiosity, did the English, or rather the Scots, have people who could spy upon foreign nations from afar? Could the Scots spy upon the English in this manner? What of the spells that protected against wounds, which were said to be used by Scottish commanders in battle (see page 66)?

This political or militaristic interest in seership, Second Sight and related matters has a long history, of course, and is by no means limited to the flurry of interest shown in the seventeenth and early eighteenth centuries. In the reign of Elizabeth I we find the great scientist and cryptographer Dr John Dee communicating with beings in other dimensions; these were spirits or angelic entities who taught him a comprehensive system of magical and spiritual arts.

Much of Dee's material has undertones similar to that described in a more humble context by Robert Kirk. Dee was for a number of years Queen Elizabeth's roving agent in Europe, and employed astrology and spirit communication to establish information, the whereabouts of hidden treasure (in England and Wales), and to develop more arcane arts pertaining to metaphysics and magic. He also drew up the maps used by the early explorers and adventurers sailing to America, based upon his navigational skills and his researches into the lost continent of Atlantis, which he assumed to be America itself. It seems very likely, though we have no proof, that his extensive cryptographic and occult skills were used, when in Europe, to pass information back to England, and perhaps to 'overlook' or spy at a distance upon the enemies of the Crown from his English house at Mortlake, and report privately to Elizabeth. We may set aside the discussion about the reality or delusion of Dee's activities, as this has been extensively covered elsewhere.[1]

More or less contemporary with Dee was the famous astrologer, doctor of medicine, and prophet, Michel de Notredame, Nostradamus. The techniques used by Nostradamus were clearly defined in his own words,[8] and far from being a Hermetic or Kabbalistic system, as we might expect from a Jewish (Christian) doctor, he uses a system of prophetic inspiration that may be traced back to both the classical Greek and Roman and ancient Celtic world. We shall return to this tradition again, for there are many implications of it in Kirk's book, and it is also found clearly described in the twelfth-century works of Geoffrey of Monmouth on Merlin, whose prophecies are similar in many ways to those later prophecies of Nostradamus. Kirk was, of course, aware of Merlin traditions and cites them in two instances (pages 32 and 62).

Many examples could be cited of a political use of esoteric arts and techniques, nowadays dignified by terms such as telepathy, and still flourishing, even advancing, in modern research. But such militaristic potential or political implications were far from the mind of Robert Kirk, for to him the Second Sight and its mysterious allies in other dimensions were not potential tools of espionage, nor were they simply barbaric or primitive superstitions, or what today we call 'folklore'. For Kirk the Second Sight and the Fairy Race were realities, though he could and frequently did make very careful distinction between such realities and common superstition or debased magical practices. Thus his work, though it never departs too far from an orthodox religious framework, is more in the tradition of Merlin, Dee and Nostradamus than we might realise at first glance.

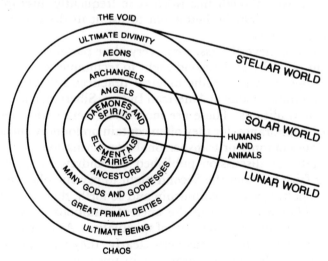

Figure 1. Human and Otherworld Entities

To this general connection we can add one of the classic examples of seership and contact with the fairy realm, that of Thomas of Earlston (Erceldoune), Thomas the Rhymer. This historical thirteenth-century poet was transported to a mysterious underground realm by a beautiful woman upon a white horse: she revealed herself to be the Queen of Elfland: he served her for seven years, and upon his return to the human world, was gifted with the power of prophecy and poetry, sometimes described as the Tongue that Cannot Lie. Many of Thomas' prophetic verses remain today, as does the long Romance poem of his underworld experience, and a ballad in Scottish-English, preserved in Lowland folk tradition until the late nineteenth century.

It is on this level of an active magical or spiritual tradition that we shall approach *The Secret Commonwealth*. In many ways the close of the twentieth century is a good time to reassess this text and present it in modern English: today there is a huge upsurge of interest and involvement in all types of esoteric and magical tradition. We can recognise much of what occurs in Kirk's book, not only as remnants of Celtic paganism, but as an account of an active initiatory tradition, related in some ways to shamanism, though this word is so frequently misapplied today that it might be better not to use it in the context of Gaelic traditions.

There are, nevertheless, some very close parallels in Kirk's account of fairies and Second Sight to techniques of shamanistic magic, and to specific magical practices still preserved and undertaken today in American Indian, Siberian, and other chthonic traditions. These are more than mere curiosities or primitive ignorance, for they often contain profoundly effective techniques of inner or transpersonal transformation.

Despite the discussion published by Andrew Lang, comparing fairy lore and the Second Sight to psychic phenomena such as poltergeists, mediumship and so forth, there are some major differences between the ancient traditions of seership and the quite modern concepts of spiritualism. As Kirk himself covers many of these areas very clearly, they will appear to the reader either in his words, or in my commentary upon certain key aspects of his text. But at this introductory stage it must be stated that the ancient traditions bring with them images, techniques, communications and philosophical or metaphysical concepts, even if in a confused or corrupted form, that are of a different order and quality from those of spiritualism.

The simplest way to put this is that the concept of bland reassuring messages from entities claiming to be our dead relatives in fantastical heavenly realms is not present in any of the pagan or pagan-Christian traditions of seership: they operate in a quite different set of metaphysical dimensions with different symbolic language. Furthermore the ancestral contacts that form an important part of such ancient lore (and may seem superficially to resemble spiritualist contacts), are not described as ethereal but contemporary stereotypes of daily life, as they are in spiritualism. They are frequently of a terrifying and cathartic nature rather than reassuring and kindly.

All of the foregoing will unfold as we progress through Kirk's text, as will other strands of magical tradition, for like all collective lore, there are several traditions interwoven almost inseparably, and coexisting quite comfortably with one another and with Christianity. The Christianity is often, as Kirk describes, and as is well known from the work of other collectors,[9] of a very unorthodox and semi-pagan nature.

THE PURPOSE OF KIRK'S BOOK

It is easy to confuse Robert Kirk's aims in writing his book with a number of quite different attitudes to fairy lore taken by modern scholars. We may, of course, dispose entirely of the Victorian and subsequent notions of pretty little fairies tripping through the grass in gossamer costumes of a mildly suggestive nature: the subterranean people, as Kirk frequently calls them, are not such, and never have been. Interestingly, Kirk does use the phrase 'Tripping Darlings' (page 58), though such usage has already been carefully qualified at the opening of his text (page 21) where he describes the ancient practice of referring to that which is powerful and potentially dangerous by kindly names. Not only did the Gaels do this, as they still do to this day in isolated regions of Scotland and Ireland, but it was common in the classical world. The term *Good Goddess* used by the Romans, for example, was often descriptive of the terrifying Queen of the Underworld, Hecate, ruler of necromancy, death, poisons, cursing, and similar forces and activities.

If we read Kirk's material carefully, and try to avoid imposing any modern retrospective attitudes upon it (a difficult but not impossible task), he presents a clear and well-defined purpose to the reader. We may begin to assess this purpose by disposing of a few of the retrospective interpretations that have occasionally been put upon *The Secret Commonwealth*.

First, Kirk is not an early experimental researcher or author groping after the yet-to-be-established disciplines of folklore. He marshals his evidence of customs, occurrences, beliefs and individual cases to support a deeply philosophical or metaphysical argument and not with the intent of making a definitive or preliminary collection of Gaelic beliefs in its own right. The techniques that Kirk uses to present his case are those of the philosopher and scholar of his period, and they are easily overlooked by the modern reader, even by the trained folklorist, as they derive from a type of classical and religious education and training in logical presentation no longer used today. We shall return shortly to the ultimate aim and nature of his argument.

Second, he is not presenting 'evidence' of the Second Sight, not even in the manner undertaken in the letter that he quotes from Lord Tarbett (pages 39–45), or in other contemporary or later collections of such evidence. The Sight itself is presented as a concomitant of the existence of the subterranean world and its inhabitants, and there is no doubt in Kirk's mind or his manner of writing as to its reality. The main discussion of the Sight is not in terms of proof or 'belief' but seeks to establish a *scientific definition* of its origins, the Sight itself being undeniably a physical and widespread occurrence. This scientific attitude has sometimes been overlooked in discussion of Kirk's text, though it is given full credit in Stewart Sanderson's introduction to the Folklore Society edition, while Sanderson tends at the same time to disregard Kirk's own stated reasons for writing *The Secret Commonwealth*. We shall return to these reasons shortly.

Kirk concludes that seership and healing powers are what we would today call genetically inherited talents. In this conclusion he precedes the work of Rudolph Steiner, who has written extensively upon such subjects, by three centuries. Kirk does not, however, consider genetic inheritance to be the sole means by which the Sight is acquired, for he describes initiatory techniques connected to it, one of which seems to be for acquiring the Sight permanently (pages 32–3) and another for a temporary experience of it (page 33). He also makes some comments upon the nature of light, and a higher order or octave of light connected to seership (pages 34–5).

This octave theory is a perennial concept, with parallels in a number of magical and philosophical texts from ancient Egypt, Plato and the Neoplatonic writers, and Kabbalistic and Renaissance Hermetic philosophers. We may also find it in a number of sources such as John Dee's *Hieroglyphic Monad* and other writings, and in the *Preface* and *Centuries* of Nostradamus, neither of which has, at first glance, any overt connection with collective or racial or folklore traditions, though the connections are present upon a deeper level than that of literary derivation. Octave theories are undergoing a considerable revival at the present time in the new wave of holistic approaches to science.

Kirk himself mentions that certain of the fairy books are similar to the abstruse Rosicrucian texts (page 27), from which we may conclude that he had some degree of familiarity with such publications. While there is no proof that Kirk is formally writing within the Hermetic tradition, and no detailed evidence that he had studied it, it nevertheless remains as an undertone in his approach to his subject material and the development and proofs of his argument. He is dealing with folklore, as we might call it today, but he approaches it from the standpoint of Renaissance theosophy.

This underlying stance in Kirk's writing leads to our third area of possible misconception, for he is not making an antagonistic or a historical or even an academic or intellectual distinction between the paganism or pre-Christian lore and customs of the Highlanders, and his own deeply Christian convictions and dedicated work. He seeks instead to synthesise these levels of belief and to argue that they are not essentially in conflict with one another. Where he encounters superstitious or debased practices he firmly criticises them, but overall he constantly seeks to find a connection and a harmonious resolution between the existence of the fairy realm and its inhabitants and the development of human society within the Christian religion.

Fourth, and most important of all, Kirk is not writing of the past or of dying traditions, and not solely of his contemporary present in which he observes or participates in seership, fairy contact and healing. He is, by his own definition (pages 90 and 95) writing for the future. He presents his examples as living evidence, stating that in the future such communication between the superterranean and subterranean worlds will be a regular and normal occurrence.

We may note in this context that he sent copies to London, especially to Mrs Stillingfleet (who was expecting her seventh child) and her husband Bishop Stillingfleet. Stillingfleet was one of those divines who sought a reconciliation between nonconformist and orthodox religion, even though he held relatively high office in the state Church and put his own career at risk by such declared concepts. We know from Kirk's own account (cited in Sanderson, pages 14–16) that the Bishop was sceptical of and opposed to Second Sight and the appearance of apparitions, but Kirk saw such things as proof of spiritual truths rather than as idle superstition or sensationalism. For Kirk, the evidence of *The Secret Commonwealth* was a way forward to unity, rather than a step backwards into ignorance. This assiduous pursuit of harmonisation of viewpoints and beliefs may have partly prompted his copying of his text for the Bishop.

This brings us to Kirk's stated purpose in writing the book, which was to counter atheism and materialism (page

47). Thus we have the remarkable situation in which a clergyman, writing in a period in which violent revolution and religious war were barely over, produces a carefully reasoned argument of the existence of another world, mirroring our own. He then proceeds to demonstrate that the unquestionable presence of the Second Sight, even in unwilling or unwitting persons, reveals this other world and its normally invisible inhabitants. This, he says, will counter the growth of atheism and materialism, for it is proof proper of many dimensions such as were believed in in earlier times.

He supports this proposal not only with the evidence from Scotland in the forms of techniques and examples, but from Biblical evidence (carefully cited in chapter and verse), and classical precedent.

There is also more than a hint that Kirk, as an Episcopalian minister albeit superficially politically reformed by a mainly Presbyterian dominance in Scotland, sought to counter some of the repressive bloodthirsty attitudes of Christian religious extremism. He felt that his proof of another dimension and its inhabitants might lead to a more civilised and truly Christian accommodation of other people's beliefs. In this sense *The Secret Commonwealth* is not only an unusual text, but probably a very daring one. Kirk's arguments are so well reasoned and so supported by Biblical precedents that it would have been difficult to accuse him of witchcraft or overt paganism, yet he steers very close to vulnerability to such charges at times, not because he is truly supporting paganism, but because his argument leads always towards religious tolerance and a theosophic or perennial spiritual viewpoint. Nothing is more hateful to the extremist than tolerance and compassion.

We find more than an echo of this situation in modern attacks by religious fundamentalists upon the esoteric occult and New Age movements, which seek, as did Kirk, to find a unity out of diversity, rather than to perpetuate a hostile and divisive enforced religion. There are times, of course, when we might wish that our modern esoteric revivalists could demonstrate even a fraction of Kirk's clarity of thought and strength of spiritual conviction and discipline.

FUNDAMENTAL CONCEPTS IN
The Secret Commonwealth

If we carefully limit ourselves to the evidence presented by Kirk in his text, including his commentary upon and disagreements with Lord Tarbett's letter on the subject, we can build a clear picture of his understanding of the fairy seership and healing traditions of the Highlanders. In the following points Kirk's text only is used, and no parallels or variants are drawn in from other sources, though these are abundant.

1. There is another world or dimension that mirrors our own: it is located underground. The cycle of energies and events in that place is a polarised image of our own, thus they have summer when we have winter, day when we have night, and so forth.

2. The inhabitants of this world are real beings in their own right, and have certain substantial supernatural powers.

3. Certain people, mainly male seers, are gifted with the ability to see such beings from the mirror- or underworld, and to receive communications from them.

4. The subterranean people are able through signs and mimicry or dramatic actions to show seers what will come to pass in the human world. It is up to the seer to develop means of interpretation.

5. Humans can and do physically transfer to the fairy- or underworld.

6. The subterranean people are linked to the land, each region having its counterpart in the underworld. Thus they are, in one respect, the *genii loci* of the ancient world.

7. The spirits of the dead and of ancestors are also found in this underworld, though they are often distinct from the Fairy Race themselves.

8. Both the subterranean people and the seers who perceive them retain fragments of ancient religious and philosophical tradition, often at variance with the religious and scientific viewpoints of the day.

9. There are spiritual or psychic healers in the human world who work through methods laid down by tradition, often using corrupted prayers and incantations to accompany their healing ceremonies. These are of a different category to the seers, and do not seem to receive aid from the subterranean or underworld fairies.

THE AIM OF THE COMMENTARY

Although *The Secret Commonwealth* is only a short book, making a detailed and properly cross-referred commentary upon Kirk's thesis would be a monumental task, fit to occupy the work of a polymath scholar, or perhaps a number of scholars from varied disciplines such as folklore, mythology, Celtic studies, and Jacobean and Carolingian literature, science and history, for a number of years. Such a project is well beyond the scope and intention of the present author.

Having considered the prospect of rendering the original text into modern English for the general reader, yet without seriously detracting from the charm and skill of the original, it remained to establish a set of parameters for commentary and occasional explanation. In the case of simple examples such as compressed phrases or period usage of terms or single words, brackets or minor alterations cleared up most of the potential obscurities quite easily. But what of the concepts?

In working through Kirk's treatise, it became clear to me that there are a number of common misconceptions concerning this book, and that I, despite my familiarity with versions of it and with the traditions which it describes, was also victim to some of these misconceptions. There is nothing like working through a text word by word, concept by concept, to reveal its true meaning, providing the exercise does not become obsessive or dogmatic; some of my conclusions are found in the Introduction.

Folklore and fairy lore is well represented in academic and popular publication, though often limited in the level of interpretation and sympathy to its inner spirit. The academic folklorist, however, has rules of a discipline to follow, and in

many cases, and for good reasons, interpretation is intentionally frowned upon and eschewed. It was the neglected inner
spirit or deeper levels of tradition, so well illuminated by
Kirk, that seem to me to demand the running commentary.
Of particular interest is the concept, not devised by me, but
stated in several places by Kirk himself, that there was an
initiatory and instructional tradition connected to seership,
and a metaphysics and philosophy of the fairy traditions.

The majority of the comments and cross-references or
comparative examples, therefore, deal with this undertone
(an apt word) of a wisdom-tradition in connection with fairy
lore. I have dealt with some of the psychological or psychic
dynamics of traditional themes elsewhere, so in this book
have limited the commentary solely to those parts of Kirk's
text which seem, either subtly, or quite openly, to assert a
perennial wisdom-tradition.

It is not too obscure a task to detect the presence of such
material; we have many fragmentary records of it from the
ancient world, from early Christian writers, from classical
Norse, Celtic and other European myths and legends, and
from archaeological evidence.

We also have a wide range of texts from the Renaissance
period onwards, in which such perennial metaphysical and
magical themes and systems are restated in various ways:
although Kirk's book is always declared to be a text or
collection of folklore, it often reads like a book on alchemy,
Renaissance theosophy, or esoteric spiritual arts. It is only
fair to state firmly at this point, that many of the medieval
and Renaissance magical and mystical texts and systems can
only be truly interpreted in the light of folklore and collective
tradition, and that scholars specialising in these texts often
totally miss their true ground of origin and their relationship
to the lore of ordinary people. So the problem cuts both ways,
subterranean and superterranean, as Kirk might say.

There are also a number of direct connections between
the material described by Kirk and primal magical arts still
practised in ethnic groups or isolated communities today. To
deal with this important area of study adequately, we would
need to add an anthropologist to our group of experts, so in

the present book these connections are touched upon not as examples of anthropological material, but only in the senses where they merge with the esoteric or perennial wisdom-traditions expressed in so many different forms through the centuries. In other words, the Gaelic seers had initiatory techniques similar to those of the Siberian shamans, though there is no suggestion that one derives in any way from the other. They rise from properties and qualities of human consciousness, particularly in relationship to the environment, a subject which Kirk himself discusses in several places.

MODERNISING THE ORIGINAL TEXT

In presenting this new edition of Robert Kirk's small but famous and influential text, I have taken the step of editing it into relatively modern English. This is by no means as simple a task as one might presume, and while it may be useful to modernise the English for the general reader, I have tried as much as possible to honour the individual style and character of Kirk's writing. Thus the modernisation is only relative, and there has been no attempt to rewrite the account in contemporary idioms which might be intellectually stylish but utterly trivial and out of keeping with the original spirit of the source material.

I have paid particular attention to Kirk's use of words and phrases that might, to the modern reader unfamiliar with seventeenth-century literary styles or language, be misleading if retained in their original form, even with modernised spelling. Kirk included a Glossary in his text, and this is retained (see Appendix 8).

Much of Kirk's account of the Second Sight and fairy lore is written in typical 'shorthand' of the period, in which the sentences are, to the modern reader, compressed, often with a number of words omitted. While this style would have posed few problems to a seventeenth-century contemporary, it tends to mislead the modern reader, and I have taken the liberty of inserting in square brackets, in the customary manner, words, and, less often, phrases, which clarify the original without imposing upon it. Those who wish to see a scholarly text of the original based upon the various source manuscripts available, should consult the Folklore Society edition, edited by Stewart Sanderson.

Robert Kirk uses an anecdotal style, typical, to my mind, of the Gaelic storyteller, with many sequences set in a rambling present tense. This does not, however, weaken or detract from the clarity of his scientific analysis and his argument, once we (modern readers) have become used to the style in which it is presented. We find a similar style in other literary examples of the period, however, so there is no firm assertion here that it derives solely from oral tradition or from Kirk's daily use of Gaelic in his isolated parish. The use of an extended present tense in storytelling is an ancient feature of oral tradition, and was carried over into literature for a number of centuries; but today it is quite unacceptable for anecdotes inserted into a general narrative or for moments of high tension to be rendered into the present tense.

Some of Kirk's very long sentences, convoluted and set all in the present, I have intentionally divided, and then rendered part or all into the more usual narrative past tense. In most cases I have preserved the present tense only where it seems to work for the modern reader, but have frequently repunctuated longer rambling sentences, dividing them into several simpler units for the sake of clarity.

I have made no attempt to 'interpret' anything written by Kirk in the process of modernisation, and have firmly resisted any temptation to move away from the original sense, even when it is too obscure to modernise fully. All such possible or probable interpretations are found in my own commentary, which follows the main text, and not in the text itself. If I have been in doubt about any sentence in the original, I have left it exactly as it was, making no changes other than to modernise the spelling or simplify the punctuation. If alterations to punctuation have seemed in danger of changing the meaning of a passage or a sentence, I have scrupulously compared them to the original text punctuation, and only reworked such areas of text when it was certain that the original meaning would not be changed or lost. It is only too easy to falsify a sentence from the writings of an earlier century by changing the punctuation or inserting a word here and there which the editor finds more favourable to his or her own theories: I have applied the usual academic disciplines that are designed to prevent a hapless editor from falling into such traps, which include those described above, and detailed cross-reference work with many large dictionaries and other texts of the same period for use of specific words and idioms. At times even this lengthy process breaks down, for language was less fixed and defined than it is today, and writers tended to create and compress freely.

For reassessment of the Gaelic words and phrases in the original text I have followed the transliterations, translations and interpretations suggested by Stewart Sanderson in the Folklore Society edition unless I have felt confident to add to them in any way from other sources or from my own knowledge of the language. They seem to have been copied literally in formal Irish script by someone with no knowledge of the language (see Sanderson, page 25), thus the manuscripts preserved today are not in Kirk's original hand, as he was fluent in speaking and writing Gaelic.

Even if we had Kirk's own original copy or copies, the orthography and grammar of Gaelic or Irish at this period was very varied indeed, and we have no way of judging the idioms or dialects prevailing in Kirk's region at the time of writing. Fortunately for this new edition the Gaelic element of the text is small, and the important but highly academic argument concerning the language is not relevant to our present purpose.

THE ILLUSTRATIONS

Kirk's original text is unillustrated, but he discusses two techniques, and reiterates variants of a typical holistic cosmology, which lend themselves to graphic form. The illustrations are not intended as dogmatic assertions of Kirk's 'meaning', nor are they necessarily the exact images that were in his own mind as he wrote, though in the case of the cosmological and natural hierarchical figures, some of our illustrations are drawn literally from his words, item by item.

Where he has indicated general models, such as the rotation of the Seasons, the Quarters, and the relationships between *daemones*, fairies, angels, and humans, the relevant illustrations show typical models employed through the centuries, with emphasis on the basic attributes known to be used in pagan and early Christian Celtic culture. Where he has described metaphysical models, such as the formation of the Septenary from the Four Elements and the Trinity, we have used simple mathematical or geometric patterns, in the time-hallowed method of magical and spiritual tuition worldwide.

Overall the illustrations are intended to help the reader not only with Kirk's text itself, but with my Commentary upon it, which selects certain of the magical and metaphysical elements of the thesis, and aims to reveal the presence of a coherent initiatory tradition within Gaelic, and indeed European, fairy lore.

The Secret Commonwealth

ROBERT KIRK'S TEXT

An Essay of the Nature and actions of the Subterranean and for the most part Invisible people, heretofore going under the names of ELVES FAUNS and FAIRIES or the like among the Low-Country Scots, and termed *hubhsisgedh, caiben, lusbarten,* and *siotbsudh* among the Tramontaines [Highlanders] or Scottish-Irish, as they are described by those who have the second sight: and now, to occasion further enquiry, collected and compared.

OF THE SUBTERRANEAN INHABITANTS

1. These siths or Fairies, which they call *sluaghmaith* or the good people: it would seem, to prevent the dint of their ill attempts: for the Irish usually bless all they fear harm of, and are said to be of a middle nature betwixt man and Angel, as were daemons though to be of old: [are] of intelligent Studious Spirits, and light changeable bodies, like those called Astral, somewhat of the nature of a condensed cloud, and best seen in twilight. These bodies are so pliable through the subtlety of the spirits that agitate them, that they can make them appear or disappear at pleasure. Some have bodies or vehicles so spongeous thin and dessicate that they are fed only by sucking into some fine spirituous liquor [essence] that appears like pure air or oil. Others feed more grossly upon the core substance of corn and liquor or on corn itself, that grows on the surface of the Earth; which these fairies do steal away,

partly invisible, partly preying upon the grain as do Crows and Mice.

Wherefore in this same age [that is, in the present time] they are sometimes heard to bake bread, strike hammers, and to do such like services within the little hillocks where they most haunt. Some whereof were old before the Gospel dispelled paganism, and in some Barbarous places as yet, enter houses after all are at rest, then set the kitchens in order, cleansing all the vessels. Such drudges go under the name of Brounies [Brownies]. When we have plenty, they have scarcity at their homes; and on the contrary, for they are not empowered to catch as much prey as they please everywhere. Their robberies notwithstanding, oftentimes [they] occasion great ricks of corn not to bleed so well, as they call it, or to prove so copious by very far as was expected by the owner.

Their bodies of congealed air are sometimes carried aloft, while others grovel in different shapes, and enter into any cranny or cleft of the Earth where air enters, [as if] to their ordinary dwellings. The Earth being full of cavities and cells, and there being no place or creature but is supposed to have other animals, greater or lesser, living in, or upon it, as inhabitants; and [there is] no such thing as pure wilderness [that is, a vacuum void or emptiness of life] in the whole Universe.

2. We then, of the more terrestrial kind, having now so numerously planted all countries, do labour for that abstruse people, as well as for ourselves. Albeit when several countries were uninhabited by us, they had their easy tillage, above ground as we [do] now, the print of whose furrows do yet remain to be seen on the shoulders of the very high hills, which was done when the champagne [that is, prime or virgin arable land] was still wood or forest.

They remove to other lodgings at the beginning of each Quarter of the year, so traversing until doomsday, being impatient of staying in one place, and finding some ease by sojourning and changing habitations, their Chameleon-like [that is, changeable of colour] bodies swim in the air, near to the Earth with bags and baggage. And at such revolutions of time, Seers or men of the Second Sight, females being but seldom so qualified, have very terrifying encounters with them, even on highways. Therefore [seers] usually shun to travel abroad at these four seasons of the year, and thereby have made it a custom to this day among the Scottish-Irish [Gaelic speaking Highlanders], to keep Church duly every first Sunday of the Quarter, to sene or hallow themselves, their corn and cattle, from the shots and stealth of these wandering Tribes. And many of these superstitious people will not be seen again in Church till the next Quarter [day] begins, as if no duty were to be learned or done by them, but the only use of worship and sermons were to save them from those [fairy] arrows that fly in the dark.

They [the fairies] are distributed in Tribes and orders; and they have children, nurses, marriages, deaths and burials, in appearance even as we [do], unless they so do for a mock-show, or to prognosticate some such things [that will come] to be among us.

3. They are clearly seen by those men of the Second Sight to eat at funerals, banquets; hence many of the Scottish-Irish will not taste meat at those meetings, lest they have communion with, or be poisoned by them. Also they are seen to carry the bier or coffin with the corpse, among the Middle-Earth men [that is, mortals] to the grave. Some men of that exalted Sight, whether by art or nature have told me that they have seen at those meetings a double-man, or the shape of the same man in two places; that is, a Superterranean and a Subterranean Inhabitant perfectly resembling one another in all points, whom he [the seer] could easily distinguish one from the other by some secret tokens and operations, and so go [directly to] speak to the [real] man his neighbour, passing by the apparition or resemblance of him.

They [the seers] avouch that every Element and different state of being, has [in it] Animals resembling those of another Element, [just] as there be fishes sometimes caught at sea, resembling Monks of [a] late order, in all their hoods and dresses. So as [a result of this resemblance] the Roman [Catholic] invention of good and bad daemons and guardian Angels [is] particularly assigned [and] is called by them [that is, the seers] an ignorant mistake sprung only from this original [resemblance or reflection of species through the Elements].

They call this Reflex-man a *coimimeadh* or Co-walker, every way like the man, as a Twin-brother and Companion, haunting him as his shadow and is oft seen and known among men, resembling the Original, both before and after the Original is dead. And [this Co-walker] was also often seen, of old, to enter a house; by which the people knew that the person of that likeness was to visit them within a few days.

This copy, Echo, or living picture, goes at last to his own herd. It accompanied that [living] person so long and frequently, for ends best known to itself, whether to guard him from the secret assaults of some of its own folks, or only as a sportful Ape to counterfeit all his actions. However the stories of old Witches prove beyond contradiction that all sorts of spirits which assume light airy bodies, or crazed bodies coacted by foreign spirits, seem to have some pleasure, [or] at least to assuage some pain of Melancholy, by frisking and capering like Satyrs, or whistling and shrieking, like unlucky birds, in their unhallowed Synagogues and Sabbaths.

If invited and earnestly required, these companions make themselves known and familiar to men, otherwise, being in a different state and Element, they neither can nor will easily converse with them.

They [the seers] avouch that a Heluo or great-eater has a voracious Elve to be his attender, called [a] *geirt coimitheth*, a joint-eater, or just-halver, feeding on the pith and quintessence of what the man eats, and that therefore he continues lean like a hawk or a heron, notwithstanding his devouring appetite.

Yet it would seem that they convey that substance elsewhere, for these Subterraneans eat but little in their dwellings, their food being exactly [that is, fastidiously] clean, and served up by pleasant children like enchanted puppets. What food they extract from us is conveyed to their homes by secret paths, as some skilful women do [convey] the pith of milk from their neighbour's cows, into their own Cheese-hold, through a hair-tedder, at a great distance by art Magic, or by drawing [from] a spigot fastened in a post, which will bring milk [from] as far off as a bull will be heard to roar. The Cheese made of the remaining milk of a cow thus strained will swim in water like cork.

The method [which] they take to recover their milk is a bitter chiding of the suspected enchanters, charging by a Counter-charm to give them back their own, in God['s], or [in] their Master's name – but a little of the mother's dung stroked on the calve's mouth before it [starts to] suck does prevent this theft.

4. Their houses (that is, the fairies') are called large and fair, and, unless at some odd occasions, unperceivable by vulgar eyes, like Rachland and other Enchanted Islands; having for light continual lamps, and fires, often seen [burning] without fuel to sustain them.

Women are yet alive who tell [that] they were taken away when in child-bed to nurse fairy [spelt *ffayrie*] children, a lingering voracious image of theirs being left in their place, like their reflection in a mirror, which, as if it were some insatiable spirit in an assumed body, made first semblance to devour the meat, that it cunningly carried by, then left the carcass as it expired, and departed thence, by a natural and common death.

The [fairy] child and fire, with food, and all other necessaries, · are set before the Nurse, as soon as she enters, but she neither perceives any passage out, nor sees what these people do in other rooms of the Lodging. When the child is weaned, the nurse either dies, or is conveyed back, or gets to choose to stay there. But if any Superterranean [that is, human] be so subtle as to practise sleights [tricks] for procuring a privacy [that is, knowledge of] any of their [fairy] Mysteries, such as making use of their ointments, which as Gyge's ring, makes them invisible or nimble, or casts them into a trance, or alters their shape, or makes things appear at a vast distance, and so forth, they smite them [the human concerned] without pain as [if] with a puff of wind. And thus [the fairies] bereave them of both their natural and acquired sights in the twinkling of an eye, [for] both those sights, where once they [are] come, are in the same organ and inseparable. Or they [may] strike them dumb.

The Tramontaines to this day put bread, the Bible, or a piece of iron, in women's bed[s] when travailing [that is, in labour] to save them from being thus stolen. And they commonly report that all uncouth unknown wights are terrified by nothing earthly so much as by cold iron. They deliver [that is, explain] the reasons to be that Hell, lying between the chill tempests and fire brands of scalding metals, and the iron of the North, hence the loadstone causes a tendency to that point, by an antipathy thereto, these odious far-scenting creatures shrug and [take] fright at all that comes thence, relating to so abhorred a place whence their torment is either begun or feared to come hereafter.

5. Their apparel and speech is like that of the people and country under which they live: so they are seen to wear plaids and variegated garments in the Highlands of Scotland and Suanochs (*sunach* or tartan) heretofore in Ireland. They speak but little, and that by way of whistling, clear, not rough. The very devils conjured in any country do answer in the language of that place, yet sometimes these subterraneans do speak more distinctly than at other times.

Their women are said to spin, very finely, to dye, to tissue and embroider; but whether it be as [a] manual operation of substantial refined stuffs with apt and solid instruments, or only curious cobwebs, impalpable rainbows, and a fantastic imitation of the actions of more terrestrial mortals, since it transcended all the senses of the seer to discern whither, I leave to conjecture, [just] as I found it.

6. Their men travel much abroad [that is far and wide], either presaging or aping the dismal and tragical actions of some among us, and have also many disastrous doings so of their own, [such] as Convocations, Wounds, and Burials, both in the Earth and Air. They live much longer than we [do], yet die at last, or at least vanish from that State [in which they live]. For it is one of their Tenets that nothing perishes, but, as the Sun and [the] Year, everything goes [around] in a Circle, Lesser or Greater, and is renewed, and refreshed in its revolutions. As it is another [tenet] that Every Body in the Creation moves, which [movement] is a sort of life, and that nothing moves but what has another Animal moving on it, and

so on, to the utmost minute corpuscle that is capable to be a receptacle of Life.

7. They are said to have aristocratic rulers and laws, but no discernible religion, love, or devotion towards God and Blessed Maker of all. They disappear whenever they hear his name invoked, or the name of Jesus, at which all do bow willingly or by constraint that dwell above or beneath [or] within the Earth (Philip 2:10); nor can they enact anything at that time, after hearing of that Sacred Name.

The *Tabhaisder* or Seer that corresponds with this kind of Familiar, can bring them with a spell to appear to himself or [to] others whenever he pleases, as readily as the Endor Witch did those of her own kind. He tells that they are ever readiest to go on hurtful errands, but seldom will be the messengers of great good to men. He is not terrified with their sight when he calls them, but seeing them by surprise, as he often does, frightens him extremely. And gladly he would be quit of such [sights], for the hideous spectacles seen among them, [such] as the torturing of some wight, earnest ghastly staring looks, skirmishes, and the like. They do not [do] all the harm which they appear to have power to do; nor are they perceived to be in great pain, save that they are usually silent and sullen.

They are said to have many pleasant Toyish Books. But the operation of these pieces [of literature] only appears in some paroxysms of antic Corybantic jollity – as if ravished and prompted by a new spirit entering into them at that instant, lighter and merrier than their own. Other Books they have of involved abstruse sense, much like the Rosicrucian style. They have nothing of the Bible, only collected parcels of Charms and counter-Charms; not to defend themselves withal but to operate on other Animals' for they are a people invulnerable by [that is, to] our weapons.

And albeit Were-Wolves and Witches true bodies are, by the union of the spirit of nature that runs through all, echoing and doubling the blow towards another, wounded at home when the[ir] astral assumed bodies are stricken elsewhere, [just] as the strings of second harp tuned to a unison sound, though only [the first] one be struck, yet these [fairy] people have not a second or so gross a body at all to be so pierced. But as air, which when divided unites again, of if (indeed) they feel pain by a blow, [then] they are better physicians than we [are], and quickly cure it. They are not subject to sore sicknesses, but dwindle and decay at a certain period, all [at] about one age.

Some men say their continual sadness is because of their pendulous state, like those men (Luke 13:26) uncertain [as to] what at the last Revolution [of the world] will become of them, when they are locked up into an unchangeable condition. And if they have any frolic fits of mirth, it is as the constrained grinning of a Mort-head [death's-head], or, rather as [it might be] acted on a stage, moved by another, [rather] than cordially coming [to laughter] of themselves. But other Men of the second sight being illiterate and unwary in their observations, vary from these [interpretations and comments].

One averring those subterranean people to be departed souls attending a while in their inferior state, and clothed with [temporary] bodies procured through their Alms-deeds in this Life called *cuirp dhaondachbach*, which means fluid active, ethereal vehicles to hold them[selves together], that they may not scatter, nor wander and be lost in the Totum [plenum or fullness], or [in] their first nothing [the Void.] But if any are so impious as to have given no alms, they say [that] when the souls of such do depart, they sleep in an inactive state until they resume Terrestrial Bodies again.

Others, those which the Lowland Scot calls a wraith, and the Irish *eug* or death-messenger, appearing sometimes as a little rough dog, and if crossed, and conjured [beneficially] in time will be pacified by the death of any other creature instead of the sick man, are only exuded fumes of the man approaching death. [These are] exhaled and congealed into a various sickness, as ships and armies are sometimes shaped in the air, and [are] called Astral Bodies, agitated as wild-fire with [the action of the] wind, and are neither Souls nor Counterfeiting Spirits.

Yet not a few vouch, as is said, that surely these are a numerous people by themselves, having their own polities [that is, systems of society and government]. This diversity of judgements may occasion several inconsistencies in this [my present] Rehearsal [of fairy lore] after the narrowest scrutiny [has been] made about it.

8. Their weapons are mostly solid earthy bodies, nothing of iron, but much of a Stone similar to yellow soft flint [and] shaped like a Barbed arrow head, but flung as a dart with great force. These arms, cut by art and tools it seems beyond human [skill], have somewhat of the nature of a thunder-bolt, subtly and mortally wounding the vital parts without breaking the skin. Some of these wounds I have observed in beasts, and felt them with my [own] hands. They [that is, fairies] are not as infallible [as] Benjamites, hitting at [that is, to within] a hair's breath; nor are they wholly unvanquishable, at least in appearance.

The men of that Second Sight do not [simply] discover strange things when asked, but at [that is, in] fits and Raptures, as if inspired with some Genius at that instant, which before did lurk in or about them. Thus have I frequently spoken to one of them who in his transport[ed state] told [that] he cut the body of one of these [fairy] people in two with his iron weapon, and so escaped this onset [of the Second Sight]. Yet he saw nothing left behind of the apparently divided body. At other times he out-wrestled some of them.

His neighbours often perceived this man to disappear at a certain place and then about one hour after to become visible [again] and discover himself [that is, reveal himself] nearly a bow-shot from the first place. It was in that place where he became invisible, said he, that those subterraneans did encounter and combat with him.

Those [mortals] who are unsanctified, called Fey, are said to be *goinnt*, that is pierced or wounded by those [fairy] people's weapons, which makes them do somewhat [that is, behave] very unlike their former habits, causing a sudden alteration, yet the cause thereof [is] unperceivable at present [that is, in the moment in which it occurs]. Nor have they the power, either they cannot make use of their natural powers, or ask not [for] Heavenly aid, to escape the impending Blow.

A man of the Second Sight perceived a person standing next to him, [and] sound [of health] to others' view, wholly gored in blood, and he [the seer], amazed like, bid him instantly flee. The whole [that is, healthy] man laughed at his art and his warning, since there was no appearance of danger; he had scarce contracted his lips from laughter, when unexpectedly an enemy leapt in at his side and stabbed him.

With their weapons they [the fairies] also *gon* or pierce cows or other animals, usually said to be Elf-shot, whose purest substance, if they [subsequently] die, these subterraneans take to live on, [which is to say] the aerial and ethereal parts, the most spirituous [of] matter for [the] prolonging of Life, leaving the Terrestrial [parts] behind; such [that is, just] as aquae-vita [distilled spirits or whisky], moderately taken, is [the purest] among liquors. The cure of such hurt is simply for a man to find out the hole [of the Elf-shot] with his finger, as if the spirits flowing from the man's warm hand were antidote sufficiently against the poisoned darts.

9. As Birds and Beasts whose bodies are much used to the change of the free and open air [thus] foresee storms, so those invisible people are more sagacious to understand by [using] the Book of Nature, things [yet] to come, than we [are], who are pestered with the grosser dregs of all Elementary mixtures, and have our purer spirits choked by them. The Deer scents out a Man, and [gun] powder though a late invention, at a great distance; a hungry hunter [scents out] bread, and the Raven [scents] carrion. Their brains, being long clarified by the high and subtle air, will observe a very small change in a trice.

Thus a Man of the Second Sight perceiving the operations of these forecasting invisible [fairy] people among us, indulged through a stupendous providence to give warnings of certain remarkable events, either in the Air, Earth, or Waters, told [that] he saw a winding-shroud creep up around a walking healthy person's legs, until it came to the knee. And afterwards it came up to the middle [of the man's body], then to the shoulders, and at last over the head, which [vision of a shroud] was visible to no other person. And by observing the space of time between the several [progressive] stages, he [the seer] easily guessed how long the man was to live who wore the [astral] shroud, for when it approached his head, he told [me] that such a person was ripe for the Grave.

10. There be many places called Fairy Hills, which the mountain people think impious and dangerous to peel or uncover by taking earth or wood from them, superstitiously believing the souls of their predecessors to dwell therein. And to that end, they say, a Mote or Mount was dedicated beside every Church-yard, to receive the souls until their adjacent bodies arise, and so [the Church's artificial mound] becomes as a Fairy-hill. [Meanwhile] they use bodies of air when called [to travel] abroad [that is, about].

They [the seers] also affirm [that] those Creatures that move invisibly in a house, and cast huge great stones, but do not much hurt because counter-wrought by some more courteous and charitable spirits that are everywhere ready to defend men, (as in Daniel 10:13) to be Souls that have not attained their rest. [Such souls are active] through a vehement desire of revealing a murder or notable injury done or received, or a Treasure that was forgot in their Lifetime on Earth, which, when disclosed to a Conjurer alone, the Ghost quite removes [itself from the site of its haunting].

In the next country [region] to that of my former residence about the year 1676, when there was some scarcity of grain, a marvellous illapse and vision strongly struck the imagination of two women in one night, [both] living at a good distance from one another, about a Treasure hid in a hill called *Sith Bhruaich* or Fairy Hill. The appearance of the treasure was first represented to their fancy, and then an audible voice named the place where it was, to their awakening senses. Whereupon both arose and meeting accidentally at the place, discovered their [mutual] design, and jointly digging, found a vessel as large as a Scottish-peck. [This was] full of small pieces of good money, of ancient coin; which halving between them, they sold in dish-fulls for dish-fulls of [grain- or oat-] meal to the country people. Very many [witnesses] of undoubted credit [that is truthfulness] saw, and have [possession] of the coins to this day; but whether it was a good or bad Angel, one of the Subterranean people, or the restless soul of him who hid it that [so] discovered it [to the two women simultaneously], and to what end it was done, I leave to the examination of others.

11. These subterraneans have Controversies, doubts, disputes, feuds, and siding of parties [against one another], there being some ignorance in all creatures, and the vastest created Intelligences not encompassing all things. As to vice and sin, whatever their own Laws be, sure[ly] according to ours, and equity natural, civil and revealed, they transgress and commit acts of injustice, and sin by what is above aids, [such] as to their stealing of nurses to [that is, for] their children, and that other sort of plaganism [theft] in catching our children away, which may seem Heir to some Estate in those invisible dominions, which [children] never return.

[As] for the incontinence [that is, unfaithfulness] of the *Leannain Sith* [fairy lemans or lovers], or succubi who tryst with men, it is abominable. But as for swearing and intemperance, they are not observed [to be] so subject to those irregularities, as [they are] to envy, spite, hypocrisy, lying, and dissimulation.

12. As our religion obliges us not to make a peremptory and [over-] curious search into these [fairy] abstrusenesses, so [we may use the examples of] histories of all ages [which] give as many plain examples of extraordinary occurrences as [may] make a modest inquiry not contemptible. How much is written of pygmies, fairies, nymphs, sirens, apparitions, which though not the tenth part [being] true, yet could not spring [out] of nothing? Even English authors relate of Barry Island in Glamorganshire, [saying] that [upon] laying your ear unto a cleft of the rock, [the] blowing of bellows, striking of hammers, clashing of armour [and] filing of irons will be heard distinctly. [This noise has occurred] ever since Merlin enchanted those subterranean wights to [make] a solid manual forging of arms to [equip] Aurelius Ambrosius and his Britains, [so binding them to labour] until he returned. [But] Merlin being killed in battle, and not coming [back] to loose the knot, these active Vulcans are there [still] tied to a perpetual labour. But [I intend] to dip no deeper into this well [of historical examples], [and] I will next give some account of how the seer, my informer, came to have this secret way of correspondence [that is, communication or vision] beyond other mortals.

There be odd solemnities at [the] investing [of] a man with the privileges of the whole Mystery of the Second Sight. He must run a tedder of hair (which bound a corpse to a bier) in a helix about his middle from end to end, and then bow his head downwards (as did Elijah, I Kings 18:42), [and] then bow his head downwards, and look back through his legs until he see a funeral advance, till the people cross two Marches; or [he may] look thus back[wards] through a hole where there was a knot of fir [in a fir-tree]. But if the wind changes point while the hair tedder is tied about him, he is in peril of his life.

The usual method for a curious person to get a transient [that is, temporary] sight of this otherwise invisible crew of Subterraneans, if impotently and over-rashly sought, is to put his foot on the Seer's foot, and [then] the Seer's hand is put on the inquirer's head, who is [then] to look over the wizard's [seer's] right shoulder. [This method is one] which has an ill appearance [for it implies] as if by this ceremony an implicit surrender were made of all between the wizard's foot and his hand before the persons can be admitted [as] a privado to the art [of seership].

Then will he see a multitude of wights like furious hardy men flocking to him hastily from all Quarters, as thick as atoms in the air. These are not nonentities or phantasms, [or] creatures proceeding from an affrighted apprehension [or] confused or crazed sense, but realities appearing to a stable man in his wakening senses and [thus] enduring [that is, undergoing] a rational trial of their being. These [beings], through fear, strike him breathless and speechless, but the seer or wizard, defending the lawfulness of his skill, forbids such horror, and comforts his novice [that is, pupil] by telling of Zacharias being struck speechless at seeing of apparitions (Luke 1:20).

Then he further maintains his art by vouching Elisha to have had the same [vision] and [that he] disclosed it thus to his servant in 2 Kings 6:17 when he blinded the Syrians, and [also] Peter in Acts 5:9, foreseeing the death of Sapphira, by perceiving, as it were, her winding sheet about her before-hand. And [the seer also cites] Paul in 2 Corinthians 12:4, who got such a vision and sight as should not, nor could, be told. Elisha, also, in his chamber, saw Gehazi his servant at a great distance taking a reward from Naaman, (2 Kings 5:26). Hence were the [Biblical] prophets

often called Seers, or men of second and more exalted sight
than others.

He [the seer] cites for his purpose also Matthew 4:8, where
the devil undertakes to give even Jesus a sight of all nations and
the finest things in the world at one glance, though in their
natural situation and station [these are] at a vast distance from
one another. And it is said expressly [that is, specifically that]
he [the devil] did let him [Jesus] see them; not in a map, it
seems, nor by a fantastic, magical juggling of the sight, which
he [the devil] could not impose upon so discerning a person
[as Jesus]. It would appear then to have been a sight of real
solid substances and things of worth, which intended as a bait
for his purpose [of temptation].

Thus it might seem, comparing this relation of Matthew
4:8. with the former [Biblical instances cited], that the extraordinary or Second Sight can be given by the ministry of bad
as well as good spirits, to those that will embrace it. And the
instances of Balaam and [of] the Pythoness make it nothing
less probable.

Also the seer trains his scholar by telling [him] of the
gradations of nature, [which are] ordered by a wise providence;
that [just] as the sight of bats and owls transcends that of
shrews and moles , so the visive [that is, visual] faculties of men
are clearer than those of owls, [and just] as [the visive faculties
of] eagles, lynxes, and cats are brighter than men's. And again
[the seer teaches] that men of the Second Sight, being designed
to give warnings against the secret engines [that is, devices and
occurrences] surpass the ordinary vision of other men, which
is a native habit in some, descended from their ancestors, but
acquired as an artificial improvement of their natural sight in
[the case of] others.

The sight of such seers resembling in their own kind [that
is, way] the usually artificial helps of optical glasses, [such]
as prospectives, telescopes, and microscopes, without which
adscititious [that is, supplementary] aids, these men here
treated of [that is, discussed] do perceive things that for
their smallness of subtlety and secrecy are invisible to others,
though [they may be] daily conversant with them. They [the
seers] having such a beam [of light] continually about them,

[such] as that of the sun, which when it shines clearly only, lets common eyes see the [dust] atoms in the air, [fragments] that without these rays they could not discern.

Some have this Second Sight transmitted from father to son through the whole family, without their own consent or the teaching of others, proceeding only from a bounty of providence, it seems, or by a compact, or a complexional quality of the first acquirer [of the sight]. As it may likewise seem strange, yet nothing vicious, in the [cases of] such as Mr Greatrakes, the Irish stroker [that is, healer], seventh sons, and others that cure the King's Evil, and chase away diseases and pains, with only [that is, nothing more than] stroking of the affected part [of the body].

Which [ability], if it be not the relic of miraculous operations, or some secret virtue in the womb of the parent, which increases until seven sons be born and decreases by the same degrees afterwards, proceeds only from the sanative [that is, curative] balsam of their healthy constitutions. Virtue goes out from them by spirituous effluxes into the patient, and their vigorous healthy spirits affecting the sick, [just] as usually the unhealthy fumes of the sick infect the sound or whole [that is, healthy].

13. The minor sort of seers prognosticate many future events, only for the space of a month [ahead], from the shoulder-bone of a sheep, on which a knife never came, for as has been said before (see page 26 above) (and the Nazarets of old had something of it), iron hinders all the operations of those that travail [that is, work] in the intrigues of those hidden [fairy] dominions. This science [of using a shoulder-blade] is called *silinnenaith*. By looking into the bone they will tell if whoredom be committed in the owner's house, what money the master of a sheep had, if any will die out of that house for that month [ahead], and if any cattle will take a trake [that is, be struck ill], as if planet-struck, called *earchal*. Then will they [the seers] prescribe a preservative and prevention.

14. A woman, seemingly an exception from the general rule [that men have the Second Sight, see page 22 above], and singularly wise in these matters of foresight, lived in Colonsay, an Isle of the Hebrides. [This incident of which I tell was] in

the time of the Marquess of Montrose [and] his wars with the Estates of Scotland, [and the woman] being notorious among many, was examined by some that violently seized the Isle. [They demanded to know] if she saw them coming or not; she said [that] she saw them coming many hours before they came in view of the isle, but earnestly looking, she sometimes took them for enemies [and] sometimes for friends. Moreover they looked [to her Second Sight] as if they went from the isle, [and] not as men approaching it, which made her not put the inhabitants on their guard.

The matter [that is, reason] was that the barge wherein the enemy sailed was [that is, had been] taken a little before from the inhabitants of that same isle, and the men [invading] had their backs towards the isle when they were plying the[ir] oars [to row] towards it. Thus this old Scout and Delphian Oracle was at last deceived and did deceive [her fellow islanders unwittingly]. Being asked who gave her such sights and warnings she said that as soon as she set three crosses [made] of straw upon the palm of her hand, a great ugly Beast sprang out of the Earth near her, and flew into the air. If what she enquired had success according to her wish, the Beast would descend calmly and lick up the crosses; if it would not succeed, the Beast would furiously thrust her and the crosses over the ground, and so vanish [back] to his place.

15. Among other instances of undoubted verity proving in thesis the being of such aerial people or species of creatures not vulgarly known, I add these subsequent relations, some whereof I have from my acquaintance with the actors and patients [that is, those actually involved], and the rest from eye-witnesses to the matter-of-fact.

The first of these examples shall be of a woman taken out of her child bed, and having a lingering image of herself substituted in her room. This resemblance decayed, died, and was buried, but the person stolen [away] returned to her husband after two years space, [and] he being convinced by many undeniable tokens that she was [indeed] his former wife, admitted her [to the] home, and had divers children by her.

Among other reports [which] she gave her husband, this was one: she perceived little [of] what they did in the spacious [fairy] house she lodged in, until she anointed one of her eyes with a certain unction [that is, ointment] that was by her, which they [the fairies] perceiving [this anointing] to have acquainted her with their actions, they fanned her blind of that eye with a puff of their breath. [But before they blinded her] she found the place full of light without any fountain or lamp from whence it did spring. This person lived in the country [region] next to that of my last residence, and might furnish matter of dispute among casuists, whether, if her husband had been [re]married in the interim of her two years' absence [in fairyland] he would have been obliged to divorce the second spouse at the return of the first.

There is an art apparently without superstition for recovering of [people] such as are thus stolen, but I think it superfluous to insert it [here].

I saw a woman of forty years [of] age, and examined her, having another Clergyman in my company, about a report of her long fasting; her name is Mcintyre. It was told by them of the house, as well as [by] herself, that she took very little or no food for several years past, that she tarried in the fields overnight, saw and conversed with a people [that] she knew not, [and], having wandered in seeking of her sheep and slept upon a hillock, found herself transported to another place before day. The woman had a child since that time, and is still pretty melancholy and silent, hardly ever seen to laugh. Her natural heat and radical moisture seem to be equally balanced, like an inextinguishable lamp, and going in a circle, not unlike to the faint life of bees and some sort of birds, that sleep all the winter over and revive in the spring.

It is usual in all magical arts to have the candidates prepossessed with a belief of their tutor's skill and abilities to perform their [magical] feats, and act their juggling pranks and legerdemain. But a person called Stewart, possessed with a prejudice against all that was spoken of this Second Sight, and living near to my house, was so put to it by a seer before many witnesses, that he lost his speech, and the power of his legs, and breathing excessively, as if expiring, because of the many fearful wights appearing unto him; the company were forced to carry him into the house.

It is notoriously known what fell tragically out with a yeoman in Killin in Perthshire, that lived close by, coming to a company within an ale-house, where a seer sat at table. At the sight of the entering neighbour, the seer started, rose to go out of the house, and being asked the reason of his haste, told that the entering man should die within two days, at which news the named man stabbed the seer, and was himself executed two days after for the fact.

A Minister [of the Church], very intelligent, but misbelieving in all such sights as were not ordinary, chanced to be in a narrow lane with a seer who perceived a wight of known visage [that is, which the seer recognised] furiously to encounter them, so the seer desired [that is, requested] the Minister to turn out of the way. [The Minister], scorning his [that is, the seer's] reason, and holding himself in the path with them, when the seer was going hastily out of the way, they were [both] violently cast aside, to a good distance, and the fall made them lame all [of] their life [thereafter]. A little [while] after the Minister was carried home, one [that is, someone] came to toll the bell for the death of the man, [he] whose representation met them in the narrow path some half an hour before.

Another example is [as follows]: a seer in Kintry, in Scotland, sitting at [the] table with divers others, suddenly did cast his head aside. The company asked why he did it; he answered that such-[and-such] a friend of his by name, then in Ireland, [had] threatened immediately [that is, at that very moment] to cast a dish-full of butter in his face. The men [who were present] wrote down the day and hour, and sent to the gentleman [in Ireland] to know the truth. Which [very] deed the gentleman declared he did at that very time, for he knew [he said] that his friend was a seer, and would [therefore know of it and] make sport with it. The men that were present and examined the matter exactly told me this story, and [said] withal, that a seer would, with all his [supernatural] optics [that is, vision] perceive no other object so readily as this at such a distance.

A succinct account of my Lord of Tarbott's [Tarbett's] relations in a letter to the Honourable Robert Boyle Esquire, of the predictions made by a seer whereof himself was ear and eye-witness. I thought fit to adjoin hereunto, that I might not be thought singular in this disquisition, that the matter of fact might be undeniably made out, and that I might with all submission give some annotations with animadversions on his supposed causes of that phenomenon, with my reasons of dissent from his judgement.

Sir,

I heard very much but believed very little of the Second Sight, yet its being affirmed by several [people] of great veracity I was induced to make enquiry after it in the year of 1652, being then confined to abide in the North of Scotland by the English usurpers. The more general accounts of it were that many Highlanders, [and] yet far more Islanders were qualified with this Second Sight, that men women and children indistinctly were subject to it, and children where parents were not: sometimes people came to age [with it] who had it not when young, nor could any tell by what means [it was] produced. It is a trouble to most of them who are subject to it and they would be rid of it at any rate if they could.

The Sight is of no long duration, only continuing so long as they can keep their eye steady without twinkling [blinking]. The hardy therefore fix their look that they may see longer, but the timorous see only glances, their eyes always twinkling at the first sight of the object.

That which is generally seen by them are the species of living creatures and of animate things which are in motion, such as ships and habits upon persons. They never see the species of any person who is already dead. What they foresee fails not to exist in the mode and in that place where it appears to them. They cannot well know what space of time shall intervene between the apparition and the real existence. But some of the hardiest and the longest [in] experience have some rules for conjectures, [such] as if they see a man with a shrouding sheet in the apparition, [then] they will conjecture at the nearness or remoteness of his death by the more or less of his body that is covered by it.

They will ordinarily see their absent friends though at a great distance, sometimes no less than from America to Scotland sitting standing or walking in the same certain place, and then they conclude with assurance that they will see them so and there. If a man be in love with a woman they will ordinarily see the species [vision or double] of that man standing by her, and so likewise if a woman be in love, and they [the seers] conjecture at their [the lovers'] enjoyments of each others by the species touching of the person, or appearing at a distance from her, if they enjoy not one another. If they see the species of any person who is sick to death they see them covered over with the shrouding sheet.

These general [instances] I had verified to me by such of them as did see and were esteemed honest and sober by all the neighbourhood, for I enquired after such for my information. And because there were more of these seers in the Isles of Lewis, Harris, and Uist than in any other place, I did entreat Sir James MacDonald, who is now dead, Sir Normand Macleud, and Mr Daniel Morrison, a very honest parson, who are [all] still alive, to make enquiry into this uncouth sight and to acquaint me therewith, which they did, and all found an agreement in these general [instances], and informed me of many [other] instances, confirming what they said. But though [they are from] men of discretion and honour, being but [reports] at second hand, I will choose rather to put myself than my friends on the hazard of being laughed at for incredible relations [that is, stories].

I was once travelling in the Highlands, and [had] a good number of servants with me, as is usual there. One of them going a little before me [and] entering into a house where I was to stay all night and going hastily to the door, he suddenly stepped back with a screech, and did fall by a stone which hit his foot. I asked what the matter was, for he seemed to be very much frightened. He told me very seriously that I should not lodge in that house, because shortly a dead [man's] coffin would be carried out of it, for [he saw] many were carrying of [and that was] when he was heard [to] cry.

I neglected his words and stayed there, [and] he said to others of the servants [that] he was sorry for it and that surely what he saw would shortly come to pass. [And] though no sick person was then there [in the house], yet the landlord, a healthy Highlander, died of an apoplectic fit before I left the house.

In the year of 1653, Alexander Monro, afterwards Lieutenant Colonel to the Earl of Dumbarton's Regiment, and I, were walking in a place called Ullapool in Loch Broom, on a little plain at the foot of a rugged hill. There was a servant working with a spade in the walk before us, [and] his back was to us, and his face to the hill. Before we came near to him he let the spade fall, and looked toward the hill; he [then] took notice of us as we passed near by him, which made me look at him, and perceiving him to stare a little strangely, I conjectured him to be a Seer. I called at [that is, to] him, at which he started and smiled. What are you doing? said I. He answered: I have seen a very strange thing, an army of Englishmen leading horses, coming down that hill, and a number of them eating the barley which is growing in the field near to the hill.

This was on the fourth of May, for I noted the day, and it was four or five weeks before the barley was sown in the field that he spoke of. Alexander Monro asked him how he knew they were Englishmen. He [the seer] said: because they were leading of horses, and had on hats and boots, which he knew no Scotsman would have there. We took little notice of the whole story as [anything] other than a foolish vision, but [we certainly] wished that an English party were there, we being then at war with them, and the place almost inaccessible for horsemen.

But in the middle of August thereafter, the Earl of Middleton, then Lieutenant for the King in the Highlands, having occasion to march a party of his towards the South Highlands, he sent his foot [soldiers] through a place called Inverlawel, and the fore-party which was first down the hill did fall of eating the barley which was on the little plain under it. Monro, calling to mind what the seer [had] told us in May preceding, he wrote of it, and sent an express [letter] to me in Loch Slin, in Ross, where I then was.

I had occasion once to be in company where a young lady was, excuse my not naming of [actual] persons, and I was told there was a notable seer in the company. I called him to speak with me, as I did ordinarily when I found any of them, and after he had answered several questions, I asked if he knew any person to be in love with that [young] lady. He said [that] he did, but he knew not the person, for during the two days [that] he had been in her company, he perceived [some-]one standing near her, and his head [was] leaning on her shoulder, which, he said, did foretell that the man should marry her, and [then] die before her, according to his observation.

This was in the year 1655. I desired him to describe the person [whom he saw], which he did, so that I could conjecture by the description of such a one [that is to, be someone] who was [indeed] of that lady's acquaintance, though there were no thought of their marriage until two years after.

And having occasion in the year 1657 to find this seer who was an Islander in company with the other person whom I conjectured to have been described by him [in 1655], I called the seer aside and asked him if that was [indeed] the person [that] he saw beside the lady nearly two years past [as described above]. The seer said it was he indeed, for he had seen that [same] lady just then, standing by him hand in hand. This [incident] was some few months before their marriage, and the man [whom the seer first described, then subsequently met two years later] is since dead, and the lady [is] still alive [as the seer had predicted in 1655].

I shall trouble you with but one more [example] which I thought [the] most remarkable of any that occurred to me. In January of 1652 the above mentioned Lieutenant Colonel Al. Monro and I happened to be in the house of one William MacLeod of FerrinLea, in the country of Ross. Monro, the Land Lord [that is, MacLeod] and I were sitting in three chairs near the fire; in the corner of the great chimney were two Islanders, who had that very night come to the house, and were related to the Land Lord.

While one of these [islanders] was talking with Monro, I perceived the other to look oddly toward me, [and] from his look, and his being an Islander, I conjectured him [to be] a seer, and asked him what he stared at? He answered by asking me to rise from the chair, for [he said] it was an unlucky one. I asked why, [and] he answered because there was a dead man in the chair next to me!

Well, said I, if he be in the next chair I may [therefore] keep my own, but what is the likeness of the [dead] man? The seer said he was a tall man with a long grey coat, booted, and one of his legs hanging over the arm of the chair, and his head hanging dead to the other side, and his arm backwards, as if it was broken.

There were some English troops quartered near that place, and there being at that time a great frost after a thaw, the country was covered all over with ice. Four or five of the English rode by this house [where we were staying], some two hours after the [seer's] vision, and while we were sitting by the fire we heard a great noise, which proved to be these troopers with the help of other servants, carrying in one of their number. He had taken a very mischievous fall, and had broken his arm, and was falling frequently into swooning fits. They brought him into the hall, and set him in the very chair and in the very posture that the seer had proposed [that is, foreseen]; but the man did not die, although he recovered with great difficulty.

Among the accounts given [to] me by Sir Normand Macleod there was one worthy of special notice, which was thus: there was a gentleman in the Isle of Harris, who was always seen by the seers with an arrow in his thigh. Such [of those dwelling] in the Isle who thought these prognostications infallible did not doubt but that he would be shot in the thigh before he died. Sir Normand told me that he heard it [to be] the subject of their discourse for many years, whenever that gentleman [with the visionary arrow in his thigh] was present.

At last the man died without any such accident, [and] Sir Normand was at his burial at Saint Clement's Church in the [Isle of] Harris. At the same time the corpse of another gentleman was brought to be buried in the very same church. The friends on either side came to debate who should first enter the Church, and in a trice from words they came to blows. One of the number who was armed with bow and arrows let fly [at] one [man] among them. Every family in that Isle has their burial place in the Church in a stone chest, and the bodies are carried in open biers to the burial place. Sir Normand, having appeased the tumult, found one of the arrows shot into the dead man's thigh. To this [event] Sir Normand himself was a witness.

In the account which Mr Daniel Morrison, [a] parson in the [Isle of] Lewis gave me, there was one [event] which, though it may be heterogeneous from this subject [of the Second Sight], yet it may be worth your notice. It was of a young woman in his parish, who was mightily frightened by seeing her own image, [standing] still before her, always when she came out into the open air. The back of the image being always to her, so that it was not a reflection as [might be seen] in a mirror, but the species [that is, vision] of such a body as her own, and in a very like habit [that is, clothing] which appeared to herself continually before her. The parson kept her a long while with him, but had no remedy of [that is, for] her evil [that is, ill] which troubled her exceedingly. I was told afterwards that when she was four or five years older, she saw it not [that is, no longer].

These are matters of fact which I assure you are truly related. But these and all others that occurred to me [that is, which I encountered] by information or otherwise, could never lead me into a remote conjecture of the cause of so extraordinary a phenomenon. [I could not decide] whether it be a quality in the eyes of some people in those parts, concurring with a quality in the air also. Whether such species [that is, visions] be everywhere though not seen by [that is, for] the want of eyes so qualified, or from whatever other cause, I must leave to enquiry of clearer judgement than mine. But a hint may be taken from this image which appeared [standing] still to the woman above mentioned, and from another mentioned by Aristotle in the fourth [book] of his Metaphysics, if I remember right, for it is [a] long [time] since I read it. And also from that common opinion that young infants, unsullied with many objects, do see apparitions which are not seen by those of elder years. Likewise from this, that several [of those that] did see [with] the Second Sight when in the Highlands or Isles, when transported to live in other countries, especially in America, they quite lost this quality. This was told me by a gentleman who knew some of them in Barbados who did see no vision there, although he knew them to be seers when they lived in the Isles of Scotland.

Thus far My Lord Tarbett (Kirk's note: his commentary follows):

My Lord, after narrow inquisition has delivered many true and remarkable observes [observations] on this subject [of the Second Sight]; yet to encourage further scrutiny I crave leave to say that:

1. But a few women are endowed with this [Second] Sight in respect of [that is, by comparison to] men, and their predictions [are] not so certain.

2. This Sight is not criminal, since a man can come by it unawares, and without his consent, but it's certain that he [will] see more fatal and fearful things than he [will] do gladsome.

3. The seers avouch that several [of those] who go to the Sith's [that is, *Sidh*], or people at rest and in respect of us in [that is, at] peace before the natural period of their life expires, do frequently appear unto them [that is, to the seers].

4. A vehement desire to attain this art [of the Second Sight] is very helpful to the enquirer, and the species [that is, vision] of an absent friend, which appears to the seer as clearly as if he had sent his lively [that is, living] picture to present itself before him, is no fantastic shadow of a sick apprehension, but a reality, and a messenger coming for unknown reasons. [It comes] not from the original similitude of itself, but from a more swift and pragmatic people [that is, the fairies], which [people] recreate themselves [that is, entertain or find recreation] in offering secret intelligence to men, though generally they are unacquainted with that kind of correspondence, as if they lived in a different Element from them.

5. Though my collections were written long before I saw [those of] my Lord Tarbett, yet I am glad that his descriptions and mine correspond so nearly [that is, closely]. The maid my Lord mentions who saw her image [standing] still before

her suiteth [that is, corresponds] with the Co-walker named in my [earlier] account [see page 23]. Which [Co-walker], some [people] at first thought might conjecture to be by the refraction of a cloud or mist as in the parallax, the whole air and every drop of water being a mirror to return the species [that is, images] of things, were our visive faculties [that is, our sight] sharp enough to apprehend them, or a natural reflection for the same reasons that an echo can be redoubled by air. Yet it were more feasible to impute this Second Sight to a quality infused into the eye by an unction; for witches have a sleeping ointment that when applied troubles their fantasy [that is, imagination or dreaming], advancing it to have [within it] unusual figures and shapes, represented to it as if it were [in] a fit of fanaticism, hypochondriac melancholy, or possession of some insinuating spirit raising the soul beyond its common strain [that is, level of existence].

If the palpable instances and realities seen and innocently objected [that is, shown] to the senses did not disprove it, and make this matter a palpable verity and no deception, [we might think it similar to the results of the witch's ointment], yet since this [Second] Sight can be bestowed without ointment or dangerous compact [that is, pact], the qualification is not of so bad an original source [as that of witchcraft]. Therefore:

6. By my Lord [Tarbett's] good leave I presume to say that this [Second] Sight can be no quality of the air, nor of the eyes, because:

6,1: [there are people] such as live in the same air and see all other things as far off and as clearly, yet have not the Second Sight.

6,2: A seer can give another person this [Second] Sight transiently [that is, temporarily] by putting his hand and foot in the posture he requires of him [see page 33].

6,3: The unsullied eyes of infants can naturally perceive no new unaccustomed object but what [that is, those which] appear to other men, unless exalted and clarified in some way as [in the Biblical example] of Balaam's ass for a time. Though in a witch's eye the beholder cannot see his own image reflected, as [he would] in the eyes of other people, so that [the] defect [that is, absence] of objects as well as [the] diversity of the subject may operate differently on several [different] tempers [that is, temperaments] and ages.

6,4: Though also some are of so venomous a constitution by being radicated [that is, rooted] in envy and malice, that they pierce and kill, like a cockatrice, whatever creature they first set their eye on the morning. So was it with Walter Graham, sometime living in the same parish wherein now I am, who killed his own cow after commending its fatness, and shot a hare with his eye having praised its swiftness. Such was the infection of an [his] evil eye, albeit this was unusual; yet he saw no object but what [ever] was obvious to other men as well as to himself.

6,5: If the [fact of] being transported to live in another country did obscure the Second Sight, [then] neither the parson nor the maid [mentioned above] needed [to] be much troubled for [that is, by] her [vision of a] reflex-self, as going from her wonted [that is, usual] home [region] would have salved [that is, healed] her fear. Wherefore:

7. Since the things seen by the seers are real entities, the presages and predictions found true, [though] but a few [are] endowed with this [second] sight, and those [are] not [people] of bad lives or addicted to malefices [that is, wrong-doing], the true solution of the phenomenon seems rather to be [as follows]. [They are the result of] the courteous endeavours of our fellow creatures in the invisible world to convince us, in opposition to Sadducees, Socinians, and Atheists, of a Deity, [and] of Spirits, [and] of a possible and harmless method of correspondence betwixt men and them, even in this life. [And to convince us] of their operations for our caution and warning, [and] of the orders and degrees of Angels, whereof one order, with bodies of air condensed and curiously shaped, may be next to man [that is, humankind], superior to him in understanding, yet unconfirmed; and of their region [of] habitation and influences on man, greater than that of the stars upon inanimate bodies. A knowledge reserved for these last atheistic ages, wherein the profanity of men's lives has debauched and blinded their understandings as to Moses, Jesus, and the prophets, unless they get [such] convictions from things formerly known, as from the Regions of the Dead.

Nor does the ceasing of the visions, upon the seer's transmigration into foreign kingdoms make his Lordship's conjecture of the quality of the air and eye [as above] a whit more
probable. On the contrary, it confirms greatly my account of
an invisible people, guardian over and careful of [the welfare
of] men. [Those fairy people] have their different offices [that
is, roles] and abilities in distant countries as appears in Daniel
10:13, etc. about Israel's, Greece's, and Persia's assistant
princes, whereof who so [of the assistant princes] prevails
gives dominion and ascendancy to his pupils [that is, peoples]
and vassals, over the opposite armies and countries. So [it is]
that every country and kingdom having their topical [that is,
local] spirits or powers assisting and governing them, [then]
the Scottish seer banished to America, being a stranger there
as well [that is, as much] to the invisible as to the visible
inhabitants, and wanting [that is, lacking] the familiarity
of his former correspondents, he could not have the favour
and warnings, [given] by the several visions and predictions,
which were once granted [to] him by those acquaintances and
favourites in his own country.

For if what he [the seer] was used to see were realities, as
I have made [clear evidence] appear [that is, prove], it were
too great an honour for Scotland to have such seldom-seen
Watchers and predominant powers over it alone, acting in it
so expressly, and [leaving] all other nations wholly destitute of
the like. Though [it might be said], without all peradventure
[that is, without being too risky], [that] all other people[s]
wanted [that is, lacked] the right key of their Cabinet, and
[lacked] the exact method of correspondence with them [that
is, the fairies], except [for] the sagacious active Scots, a [great]
many of whom have retained it [that is, the Second Sight] for
a long time, and by surprises and Raptures do often foretell
what, in kindness, is really [that is, truly] represented to them
at several occasions.

To which purpose the learned lynx-eyed Mr Baxter [com-
menting] on Revelation 12:7, writing of the fight between [the
Archangel] Michael and the Dragon, gives a very pertinent
note as follows: That he knows not but ere [that is, knows
no example of] any great action [that is, battle], especially

tragical, [that] is done on Earth, [but] that first the battle and [its] victory is acted [out] and achieved in the Air, between the Good and Evil Spirits. Thus he [states].

It seems [therefore] that these [visions] were man's guardians, and the like [that is, similar] battles are often times perceived aloft [in the sky] in the night time. The event of which might easily be represented by some one of the [spirit or fairy] number to a correspondent on Earth. [Just] as frequently the report of great actions [battles] has been carried more swiftly to other countries than all the art of us mortals could possibly dispatch it. St Augustine [commenting] on Mark 9:4, gives no small intimation of this truth, averring that Elias appeared with Jesus on the Mount in his proper body, but Moses [appeared] in an aerial body [which he had] assumed [that is, taken on]. [Moses' aerial body was] like [those of] the Angels who appeared and had the ability to eat with Abraham, though no necessity, on the account of their bodies, as likewise the late doctrine of the preexistence of souls, living into aerial vehicles. [These examples] give a singular hint of the possibilities of the thing, if not a direct proof of the whole assertion; which [may] yet, moreover, be illuminated by diverse other instances of the like nature, and [just] as wonderful, beside what is [said] above. [Such] as:

8. The invisible wights which haunt houses seem rather to be of our subterranean inhabitants, which appear often to men of the Second Sight, than [to be] evil spirits or devils. Though they throw great stones, pieces of earth, and wood, at the inhabitants, they hurt them not at all, [just] as if they acted not maliciously like devils, but in sport like buffoons and drolls.

All ages have offered some obscure testimonies of it [that is, the existence of otherworldly beings] such as Pythagoras' Doctrine of Transmigration; Socrates' Daemone that gave him precautions of future dangers; Plato's classing them into various vehiculated species of Spirits; Dionysius Areopagita's marshalling [of] nine orders of Spirits [from] Superior [to] Subordinate; the [classical] poets [in] their borrowing from the philosophers, and adding their own fancies of Fountain, River, and Sea Nymphs, Wood, Hill, and Mountain inhabitants, and that every place and thing in cities and countries had Special Invisible Regular Gods and Governors.

Cardan speaks of his father seeing the species [vision] of his friend on a moonlit night riding fiercely by his window on a white horse on the very night his friend died at a vast distance from him, [yet] by which [vision] he understood that some [such] alteration would suddenly ensue. Cornelius Agrippa and the learned Doctor Moore have several passages tending that [same] way.

The Noctambulos [that is, sleep-walkers] would appear to have some foreign [that is strange] joking spirits possessing and supporting them, [such as] when they walk on deep waters and tops of houses without danger, when asleep, and in the dark. For it is [in] no way probable that mere apprehension and strong imagination [could be the cause of] setting the animal spirits [of the human constitution] working to move the body. [Nor could the animal or vital energies] preserve it from sinking in the depth or falling down headlong when asleep, any more than when awake, the body being then as ponderous as before. And it is hard to attribute it to a spirit flatly Evil and Enemy to man, because the Noctambulo returns to his own place *safe*.

And the most furious tribe of the Daemons are not permitted by providence to attack men so frequently either by night or by day; for in our Highlands, as there be many fair ladies of this aerial order [of spirits or fairies] which do often tryst with lascivious young men in the quality [that is, role or guise] of succubi or lightsome paramours and strumpets. [These] are called *Leannain Sith* [fairy lemans or lovers] or Familiar Spirits [as in Deut. 18: 10–11. So do many of our Highlanders, as if strangling by the night Mare, pressed with fearful dream, or rather possessed by one of our aerial neighbours, rise up fiercely in the night and apprehending the nearest weapons do push and thrust at all persons in the same room with them, sometimes wounding their comrades to death. The like of this fell sadly out within a few miles of me at [the time of] the writing of this.

I [will] add but one instance more of a very young maid, who lived near to my last residence. In one night [she] learned

a large piece of poetry by the frequent repetition of it, from one
of our nimble courteous spirits; a part of this poem was pious,
[but] the rest superstitious, for I have a copy of it. Yet no other
person was ever heard to repeat it before, nor was the maid
capable to compose it of her self.

9. Having demonstrated and made evident to sense this
extraordinary vision of our Tramontaine [Highland] seers
and what is seen by them, by what is said above; many
having seen the same spectres and apparitions at once having
the visive faculties entire, for *non est disputandum de gustibus*. It
now remains to show that it is not unsuitable to Reason, nor
to Holy Scriptures.

9,1: First that it is not repugnant to Reason does appear
from this: that it is no less strange for Immortal Sparks
and Souls to come and be immersed into gross Terrestrial
Elementary bodies, and be so propagated, so nourished, so
fed, so clothed as they are, and breathe in such an air and
world prepared for them than for Hollanders or Hollow-cavern
Inhabitants to live and traffic among us in another State of
Being without our knowledge. For Raymond de Subunde in
his third book Chapter 12 argues quaintly that all sorts of
living creatures have a happy rational polity of their own with
great contentment, which government and mutual converse of
theirs, they all pride and plume themselves [on], because it is
as unknown to mankind as mankind's is to them.

Much more that the Son of the Highest Spirit should assume
a Body like ours, convinces all the world that no other thing
that is possible need be much wondered at.

9,2: The Manucodiata or Bird of Paradise, living in the
highest region of the air; Common Birds in the Second Region;
Flies and insects in the Lowest; Men and Beasts on Earth's
Surface; Worms, Otters, Badgers, and Fishes under the Earth
and Waters. Likewise Hell is inhabited at the Centre [of the
Earth] and Heaven in the Circumference; can we then think
the middle cavities of the Earth to be empty?

I have seen in Wemyss, a place in the County of Fife in
Scotland, divers caves cut out, as [if they are] vast Temples
under ground; the like is [also found] in a County of England.
In Malta is a Cave wherein stones of a curious cut are thrown

[up] in great numbers every day. So I have had barbed arrow-heads of yellow flint, that could not be cut so small and neat [out] of so brittle a substance by all the art of men.

It would seem therefore that these works mentioned were done by certain spirits or pure organs, and not by devils, whose continual torments could not allow them so much leisure. Beside these I have found five curiosities in Scotland, not much observed to be [known] elsewhere:

1. The brownies who in some families [labour] as drudges [and] clean the houses and dishes after all [mortals] go to bed, and removing before daybreak [each Brownie] taking with him his portion of food [as left for him].

2. The Mason Word, which though some make a Mystery of it, I will not conceal a little of what I know; it is like a Rabbinical tradition in [the] way of comment on Iachin and Boaz, the two pillars erected in Solomon's Temple, with the addition of some secret sign delivered from hand to hand, by which they [the Masons] know and become familiar with one another.

3. This Second Sight so largely [that is, extensively] treated of before.

4. Charms and curing by them very many diseases, sometime by transferring the sickness to another [carrier or location].

5. A [human] being proof of [that is, against] lead, iron, and silver, or a brief [garment] making men invulnerable. Divers of our Scottish commanders and soldiers have been seen with blue marks only, [even] after they were shot with leaden ball; which seems to be an Italian trick, for they seem to be a people too curious and magically inclined.

Finally Irish-men, our Northern Scottish, and our Atholl men are so much addicted to, and delight in, Harps and Music, as if like King Saul they were possessed with a foreign spirit. [Their possession is] only with this difference, that music did put Saul's play-fellow asleep, but roused and awakened our [Scots] men, vanquishing their own spirits at pleasure, as if they were [made] impotent [by the effect] of its powers and unable to command it. For we have seen poor beggars of them [that is, Highlanders] chattering their teeth for [that is, with] cold, that how [that is as] soon as they saw the fire and heard the harp, leapt through the house like goats or satyrs.

[Just] as there are parallel stories in all countries and ages, reported of these obscure people, which [tales] are no dotages [that is, not weak-minded], so it is no more of necessity to us to know their Beings and manner of Life than [it is] to understand distinctly the polity [that is, political organisation or statehood] of the nine orders of Angels, or with what oil the Lamp of the Sun is maintained so long and regularly; or [to know] why the Moon is called a great Luminary in Scripture, while it only appears to be so; or if the Moon be truly inhabited because telescopes discover seas and mountains in it, as well as flaming furnaces in the Sun. Or why the discovery of America was looked on as a fairy-tale, and the reporters of it hooted at as inventors of ridiculous Utopias, or the first probable asserters punished as inventors of new gods and worlds. Or why, in England, the King cures the Struma by stroking, and the Seventh Son in Scotland, whether his temperate complexion conveys a Balsam, and [so] sucks out the corrupting principles by a frequent warm sanative contact. Or whether the parents of the Seventh Child put forth a more eminent virtue to his production than to all the rest, as being the high water mark, Meridian, and height to which their vigour ascends, and from that [height] further have a gradual declining into a feebleness of the body and its productions. And then:

Q 1. Why is not the Seventh Son infected himself by that contagion he extracts from another?

Q 2. How can once or twice stroking with a cold hand have so strong a natural operation, as to exhale all the infectious warming corroding vapours?

Q 3. Why may not a Seventh Daughter have the same virtue? So that it appears, albeit a happy natural constitution concurs, yet something is in it [that is] above Nature.

Therefore every age has some secret left for its discovery, and who knows but this intercourse between the two kinds of rational inhabitants of the same Earth may be not only believed shortly [that is, soon], but as freely entertained and as well known as now [are] the art of navigation, [or] printing, gunning, riding on saddles with stirrups, and the discoveries of microscopes, [all of] which were sometimes as great a wonder and hard to be believed [in].

10. Though I will not be so curious nor so peremptory as he who will [seek to] prove the possibility of the Philosopher's Stone from Scripture, [as in] Job 28:1,2 [or] Job 22:24–25, or [to prove] the plurality of Worlds from John 14:2, and Hebrews 11:3; or [to attempt to prove] the circulation of the blood from Ecclesiastes 12:6; nor the Talismanical Art from the blind and the lame mentioned in 2 Samuel 5:6. Yet I humbly propose these passages which may give some light to our subject at least, and show that this polity and rank of [subterranean or fairy] people is not a thing impossible, nor [is] the modest and innocent scrutiny of them impertinent or unsafe.

The Legion or brigade of spirits, mentioned [in] Mark 5:10, besought our Saviour not to send them away out of that country, which shows [that] they were Daemones Loci, Topical Spirits, and peculiar superintendents and supervisors assigned to that province. And the power of the Nation granted, Revelation 2:26, to the conquerors of vice and infidelity sound somewhat to the same purpose. Tobit had a Daemon attending marriage, Tobit 3:8, and in Matthew 4:5, an evil spirit came in visible shape to tempt our Saviour. [Jesus] himself denied not the sensible [that is, to the senses] appearance of ghosts to our sight, but said [that] their bodies were not composed of flesh and bones as ours [are], Luke 24:39. In Philipp 2:10 our very subterraneans are expressly said to bow to the name of Jesus.

Elisha saw Gehazi not only intellectually [that is, in the mind] but sensibly [that is, with the eyes], when [he was] out of reach of an ordinary view. It wants not good evidence that there are more managed by God's spirit, Good, Evil, and Intermediate Spirits among men in this world, than we are aware of. The Good Spirits ingesting fair and heroic apprehensions and images of virtue and the Divine life, thereby animating us to act for a higher happiness according to our improvement. And [the good spirits] relinquishing us as strangely upon our neglect [of virtue], or our embracing the deceitful Siren-like pictures and representations of pleasures and gain presented to our imaginations by evil and sportful angels to allure us to an unthinking ungenerous and sensual life. None of [these spirits] having power to compel us to any misdemeanour without our flat consent.

Moreover, this life of ours being called a warfare, and God saying that at [the] last there will be no peace for the wicked; our busy and silent companions also being called *siths* or people [of peace] at rest and quiet in respect of us [proves their good intent]. And [there are] withal many ghosts appearing to men that want [that is, do not have] this Second Sight, in the very shapes and the speaking the same language [as] they did when incorporate and alive with us. [This is] a matter of an old imprescriptable tradition, [as] our Highlanders make still a distinction between *Sluagh Saoghalta* and *Sluagh Sith*, averring that the souls [of mortals] go to the Sith [*Sidh* or fairy hills] when dislodged.

Many real treasures and murders are discovered by souls that pass from among ourselves or by the kindness of these our Airy Neighbours, none of which spirits can be altogether inorganical. [These are] no less than the conceits about Purgatory or a State of Rescue, the Limbuss Patrum and Infantum, [which] though misapplied, yet are not Chimeras or altogether groundless. For, *ab origine*, it is [likely that these concepts are] nothing but some pale and faint discoveries of the Secret Republic of ours, [as] here treated on, that are described with additional fictions of monks, [who are] doting and crazy-heads. [For] our creed says that our Saviour descended to the house of Hades, to the Invisible place and people.

And many divines suppose that the Deity appeared in a visible shape seen by Adam in the cool of the day, speaking to him with an audible voice, and [that] Jesus, probably by the ministry of invisible attendants, conveyed more meat [that is, substance] of the same kind to the five thousand that were fed by him with a very few loaves and fishes, for a new Creation it was not. The Zijim-jiim and Ochim in Isaiah 13:21–2 [are another example for] those satyrs and doleful unknown creatures of islands and deserts seem to have a plain prospect that way. Finally the eternal happiness enjoyed in the third Heavens being more mysterious than most men take it to be, it is not a sense wholly adduced to Scripture to say that this Second Sight, and the due objects of it, has some vestige [of evidence] in Holy Writ; but rather [that] it is modestly deduced from it.

It only now remains to answer the most obvious objections against the reality and lawfulness of this speculation (such) as:

Question 1. How do you salve this Second Sight from [the accusation of diabolical] compact and Witchcraft?

Answer. Though this correspondence with the intermediate unconfirmed people [existing] between Man and Angel be not ordinary to all of us who are superterraneans, yet this Sight, falling to some person by accident, and it being co-natural to others from their birth, cannot always be derived from wickedness. Too great a curiosity to acquire [such] an unnecessary art may indeed be blameworthy; but divers of that Secret Commonwealth may by permission discover [that is, reveal] themselves as innocently to us who are in another State [of existence], as some of us men do to fish which are in another Element, when we plunge and dive into the bottom of the Seas, [which are] their native region. In the process of time we may come to converse as familiarly with those nimble and agile clans, but with greater pleasure and profit, as we do now with the Chinese and Antipodes.

Question 2. Are they [as] subject to vice, lusts, passion, and injustice as we [are] who live on the surface of the Earth?

Answer: The Seers tell us that these wandering aerial people have not such an impetus and fatal tendency to any vice as men [do]; for they are not drenched into so gross and dreggy bodies as we [are] But [they are] yet in an imperfect state, and some of them make better essay [that is, attempts] for heroic actions than others, having the same measures of Virtue and Vice as we, and still expecting advancement to a higher and more splendid state of Life. One of them is stronger than many men, yet [they] do not incline to hurt mankind, except by commission for a gross misdemeanour, as [in the case of] the destroying Angel of Egypt and the Assyrians, [in] Exodus 12:29, and 2 Kings 10:35.

They haunt [that is, inhabit] most where there is most barbarity [that is, in isolated non-English-speaking regions], and therefore our ignorant Ancestors, [in order] to prevent the insults of that strange people, used rude and coarse remedies, such as Exorcisms, Donations, and Vows. But as soon as true piety prevailed in any place, it did put the inhabitants beyond the reach and authority of subtle inferior [that is, underground] co-habitants and colleagues of ours, [for it is] The Father of All Spirits and the person himself [that] has the only [true] command of his soul and actions. A concurrence they [the fairy people] have to what is virtuously done, for upon committing of a foul deed, [a mortal] one will find a demur upon his Soul, as if his cheerful Colleague had deserted him.

Question 3. Do these aerial tribes procreate? If so, how are they nourished, and at what period of time do they die?

Answer. Supposing all Spirits to be created at once in the beginning, Souls to pre-exist, and to circle about into several states of probationship [and] to make them either totally inexcusable or perfectly happy against the last day, salves all the difficulty [of this discussion]. But [it must be argued] in every deed, and speaking suitably to the nature of things; there is no more absurdity for a Spirit to inform an infant Body of Air than a Body composed of dull and drowsy Earth, the best of spirits having always delighted more to appear into aerial than into terrestrial bodies.

They feed mostly on quintessence and ethereal essences, the pith and spirits only of women's milk feeds their children, being artificially conveyed, [just] as air and oil sink into our bodies, to make them vigorous and fresh. And this shorter way of conveying a pure aliment, without the usual digestions, by transfusing it and transpiring through the pores into the veins and arteries and vessels that supply the body is nothing more absurd than [that of] an infant being fed by [through] the navel before it is born. Nor [is it more unlikely] than a plant which grows by attracting a lively juice from the Earth through many small roots and tendons, whose coarser parts being adapted and made co-natural to the whole, do quickly coalesce by the [action of] ambient cold, and so are condensed and baked up into a confirmed wood in the one [plant] and [into] solid flesh and bone in the other [that is, the infant].

A notion, which if entertained and approved, may show that the late invention of soaking and transfusing not blood but ethereal virtual spirits, may be useful for both nourishment and health. There is a vestige of this in the damnable practice of evil Angels, [in] their sucking of blood and spirits out of witches' bodies till they drain them into a deformed and dry leanness, to feed their own [body or] vehicles withal, [so] leaving what we call the witches' mark behind. [This is] a spot, that I have seen, as a small mole, horny and brown coloured; through which, when a large brass pin was thrust, either in buttock, nose, and roof of the mouth, until it bowed and became crooked, the witches, both men and women, neither felt a pain nor did bleed, nor knew the precise time when this [action] was done to them, their eyes only being covered.

Now the air being given a body as well as Earth, no reason can be given why there may not be particles of a more vivified Spirit form of it for procreation, than is possible to be [formed] of Earth which takes more time to rarefy and ripen before it can come to have a prolific virtue. And if our Tripping Darlings did not thus procreate, their whole number would be [so] exhausted after a considerable space of time. For though they are of more refined bodies and intellectual [capacity] than we [are], and of far less heavy and corruptive humours, which are a cause of dissolution, yet many of their lives being dissonant to right reasons and [to] their own laws, and their [bodily] vehicles being not wholly free of lust and passion, especially of the more haughty spiritual kind, they pass, after a long healthy life, into an Orb and Receptacle fitted for their [proper] degree, until they come under the General Cognisance of the last day [of Judgement].

Question 4. Does the acquiring of this Second Sight make any change on the acquirer's body mind or actions?

Answer. All uncouth sights enfeeble the Seer. Daniel, though familiar with divine visions, yet fell frequently down without strength, when dazzled with a power which had the ascendant of him, and pressed on him beyond his comprehension, [as in] Cappadocians 10:8,17. So our seer is put in a rapture, transport, and sort of death as [if] divested of his body and all it senses, when he is first made participant of this curious piece of knowledge. But it makes no ramp or strain in the understanding of any [one], [but] only to the fancies of clownish and illiterate men [does] it create some affrightments and disturbance, because of the strangeness of the [vision] shows, and their unacquaintedness with them.

And as for their life, the persons endowed with this rarity are for the most part candid honest and sociable people. If any of them be subject to immoralities, this abstruse skill is not to be blamed for it, for unless [they] themselves be the tempters, the colonies of the invisible plantations with which they do intercommunicate do not provoke them to villainy or maleficence, neither at their first acquaintance, nor after long familiarity.

Question 5. Does not Satan interpose in such cases by many subtle unthought-of insinuations, as [he did] to him who let the fly or Familiar go out of the box, and yet found a fly of his own putting-in as serviceable as the other would have been?

Answer. The goodness of the life and designs of the ancient Prophets and Seers was one of the best proofs of their mission. Nor have our Seers bad lives and designs as Necromancers, as those that traffic with Devils usually have. Our Seers moreover do seldom perform any odd thing themselves, but see [by Second Sight] what is done by others. [If all of] which was acted by spirits flatly evil, [then] their aim could not but appear by [demonstration of] some extravagant work or maleficence of the Seers; yet it is well known everywhere that our Seers are [in] no way scandalous men.

Objection 6. That this Second Sight was not an art or faculty in use, or of good fame among men, or recommended of God.

Answer. Every unusual art or science is not sinful or unlawful unless its original or principal design does make it so; nor was God always pleased to discover [reveal] even every necessary truth at once, yet when such truth and science were permitted, recommended or suggested, [then] they were truly lawful. It was long time before the Jews thought it lawful to war on the Lord's day, and the religious Jews themselves were long without a distinct knowledge of the Son of God and of the Holy Ghost; yet because of the noble design of the discovery it ought not to be rejected when further revived.

Objection 7. If it is not diabolic, [then] it is no reality but a [false] apprehension.

Answer: That this species of vision is real and not fanatic is evident from the enquirer's conviction of the truth of it, though he came to the Seer possessed with prejudice, and with a previous misbelief of the art. This qualification [of disbelief] usually mars the effort of all jugglings and deceitful tricks.

[This is] not to say that the alleged Speculum Trinitatis by which every creature is seen in the Divine Essence, which some call the Beatific Vision, gives [us] some light and probability upon this branch or beam of [supernatural] Vision. Surely Elisha's servant having his eyes opened, as in 2 Kings 6:17 and seeing the mountains full of horses and chariots of the Heavenly Host, shows that there is a Sight beyond ordinary [sight], acquirable even on Earth, by infusing some quality in the eye. [And it also shows] that Intelligences traverse daily among us on Earth, directing, warning, or encamping about the faithful, though unknown and unseen to most men that live [on it].

Objection 8. The having of the Second Sight, though from the parents, being a voluntary act, and having no natural dependence of cause and effect, is therefore sinful. The curious desire to know it or put it in[to] practice, being [of itself] a believing in the Art and trusting to it, is an unusual gift, magical, not from the Beginning, and has neither a precept of God in Scripture nor promise of blessing in the exercise (thereof).

Answer: [As] to those children on whom the Second Sight descends from their parents, it is no voluntary act, but forced upon them; and as for a dependence between cause and effect, the cure of the King's Evil by the King from his ancestors, Edward the Saint, downwards, and always by the seventh son is a real effect, but depends not upon a natural cause known to us, and yet it is not scandalous nor [is it] sinful. Yawning is voluntary, yet [it] affects others by imitation, and does so innocently. So does the Loadstone attract steel necessarily, but we do not know the dependence of these effects from their natural causes; yet they are either harmless in themselves or profitable.

For trusting to the art and believing of it, the Seers cannot but believe [that] there is such an art when many infallible instances [are] presented to their senses, [and] do convince them of the reality. And yet they do not trust to it, for they, for the most part, neither seek to [acquire] the art, nor expect any advantage or pleasure by it, either in the way of enriching themselves or [of] revenge upon others. And furthermore, a person may be sinfully curious of a real and honest art, which by accident, being useless and spending too much time [upon the matter] may become sinful to him. As to a promise of blessing upon having the sight, it not being an article of faith, a matter of Salvation, or [of] necessity, but only [being] as another art of sciences lately [recently] invented, which shortly may become a profitable and pleasant speculation, it needs no more an express precept or promise than many other laudable actions and contemplations.

It needs no more [of] an express [that is, particular] precept or promise than many other laudable actions and contemplations, undoubtedly, providing our belief [in God] be firm and our actions otherwise virtuous and devout. [In such circumstances] it could not endanger our salvation, [even] though we knew not that there were such things in the universe as a crew of malicious devils; yet it is [in] many ways profitable for us to know so much which is patent and exactly applicable to our present case, as to our conjunct inhabitants of this Earthly Foot Stool [that is, the fairies].

Objection 9. That the [fact of] proceeding from their forefathers does not diminish the sin or scandal of the Second Sight, [any] more than Original Sin and other voluntary sins, as well as those of ignorance, are innocently derived from our progenitors.

Answer. Albeit Original Sin and its fatal consequence be not innocently derived to us from our progenitors, because of his Maker's Covenant with Adam for himself and his posterity, as to standing, or falling; yet this does not make hereditary diseases and all other things of our immediate parentage sinfully to affect us. It might have been a sin of intemperance and riot in the parents that entailed a radicated [that is, deep-rooted] inveterate distemper and bodily disease

in the progeny; which [of itself] is not a sin, but [an] affliction
of the children [concerned].

It is the nature of a thing [in] itself in question, and not the
manner of its derivation and other accidental concomitants,
which makes it faulty. If parents had this Second Sight by
contract with evil spirits, [then] it were [an] error on [the
part of] the first concoction which would still increase as
it proceeded forwards, among their successors. But by [the]
undeniable proofs [offered] above, I have made it appear
[clearly] that both young children and aged persons have
had this Sight infused in a trice, [and] they know not whence,
though they neither concurred to it themselves, nor any of their
parents and other relations [have] had the like before them. So
that the spies and aerial intelligences seen are real intelligent
creatures, and the sight of the seers of them [is] clear and
lawful, and void of deception; *Quod erat demonstrandum*.

CONCLUSION

Thus far [we have come in our account of] the lychnobious
people, their nature, constitutions, actions, apparel, language,
armour, and religion; [along] with the qualities of those am-
phibious seers that correspond with them. [And we have
summarised] what is said of their procuration among themselves, which is done at the consent of their wills, as one candle
lights another; and of the conjunction of their females, called
Leannain Sith or fairy lemans, like the succubi mention of old,
with superterraneans, [and] of their Merlin-like monstrous or
giant productions thereupon. And of the infrequency of their
visits and fearful appearance nowadays, as being out of their
proper Element, except [when] they be sent as a portent of
some extraordinary occasion.

Since the [spread of] the Holy Gospels flourishing among
us, in respect of their hauntings before [such] time, who, as
strangers and enemies invading other territories, left a fear of
travelling in the dark in the minds of men that dread mischief
of them. Indeed, even persons having the Second Sight, and
seers themselves, the persons most conversant with them, find

such horror and trouble by the intercourse [with them] that they would often fully [and] gladly be as free from them as [are] other men. The pursuit of all of these at more length than I now have time for, I leave to the judgement and credit of everyone else's enquiry and experience.

A SHORT TREATISE ON THE
SCOTTISH-IRISH CHARMS AND SPELLS

It is not well known when and by whom this art of charming among the Scottish-Irish was first invented and broached: but surely most of the spells relate to something in the Christian religion; some of them have words taken out of the Holy Bible as [from] Palms 50:18 [or] John 1:1, etcetera.

1. Those that defend the lawfulness of charms call them a continued miracle, which by Heaven's compassion towards mankind's infirmities, convey virtue from all the hands [that] they pass through. [This virtue is] by reason of the sanctity of the first deviser, and [they continue] to work in their own kind, as a once-dedicated Telesm [does] in its own; both lasting in vigour for many ages. And they [the charmers] give that ancient instance in Psalm. 58:4 of enchanting the adder from doing hurt, for a precedent. Albeit assuredly charmers be flatly discharged in Deuteronomy 18:11, and [therefore] reckoned up with Necromancers, witches, and consulters with familiar spirits. By experience it is found that such as come once on their reverence can never be rid of them, but will still have occasions that will need these white witches' assistance, in curing of one, when they kill another.

And yet that the Holy Scriptures may borrow a comparison of obstinacy from the asp, as well as a caveat of wariness and wit from a thief in the night, and an unjust steward, need not be wondered at.

2. There be charms for all common diseases from top to toe, from the falling evil and convulsion of the sinews to the wen and excrescence on the eye-brow called *ceannaid*. Most of them are in the way of prayers called *orrtha*, but said to be of more efficacy than any prayer now pronounced. The words,

notwithstanding [this tradition of power and sanctity] are much corrupted in [the] process of time, by being transmitted through so many mouths; and it is not easy to reconcile them all to good sense, or [give] a meaning proper for the designed conveyance [of benefit]. Besides that they are used by many of bad conversations, and who do not understand much of what they utter. [All of] which makes others to suspect that the good words and the spells are but the policy of the Counterfeit Angel of Light to lead on the unwary to his lure, and that they being intended only as a watchword and sign of the compact with his followers, he [Lucifer] is not scared to hear so many pious phrases [which are] wanting the [proper] understanding and affection, which is the life of all [prayers]. Especially since he was prompt enough to adduce Scriptural words to our Saviour himself, [as] in Matthew 4:3.

As [the spells] are spoken by rote [that is, learned by heart], so several of them were set down in rhythm [rhyme]. It was customary also with ancient practised magicians, for solemnity's sake, and to strike a greater reverence in the receivers of benefit by them, to exchange the names of ordinary things with those of creatures that had some like-operation to that which they designed to bestow. Thus [they were] framing a Sacred peculiar style of their own, which did not alter the nature of anything they spoke of, to any that could discern and distinguish, [any] more than the blessed Jesus, calling Bread his Body, changed the true nature of either, as some might [give as] instance now for their purpose [of maintaining the contrary].

Then these words so consecrated were thought operative to all that gave credit to them and were their partisans, being once made partakers of their influence. Even the Platonists in their Rites of Lustrations and purifying gave benefits, mystically signified under words of several [levels or transpositions of] representation. These words, they thought, were introduced by the gods, who knew the nature of things, and were [then] delivered by them to the first men that lived, who were called the sons of the gods, and giants, as opposed to the Filii Terrae, [who were] idiots and weaklings. [These sons of the gods], as immediately formed, and then instructed by Them, [had from] hence the sacred language of their Mysteries, [which] was believed to have Magical force from the Gods, to do the Deed [required of it]. This strong and vigorous force, but secretly conveyed, was restrained to those very words and points as delivered by tradition, without any voluntary alteration, and they [the magicians] reckoned their virtue evaporated and was lost by being poured out and translated into any other language.

The Jews also are very shy in translating any of the common forms of Blessing, or the like, prescribed in the Law by mystical ways. Both the good spirit and image of Jesus' holy mind and life, and also the malice of the evil spirit against all good, are conveyed to men according to their different endeavours after [such things]. It is not the natural influence that the pronunciation of such words can have on the things signified by them which brings their effect to pass, but purely the Promise and authority of the first institutor on such persons and things as he has command over, and manifest it [as] his pleasure so to bestow his power. Thus in a stable legal sense, every office has its *vocabula artis*, whose property is understood according to the occupation it treats about [that is, describes], whether sacred, civil or profane. Just as what is cloth in the merchant's hand is [then] called a cloak or coat when [it has] come through the hands of the tailor.

There be philtres used and other attractives of love, by spells or words, as well as by other meretricious arts, that cause the persons [so] beloved, if but touched, to follow the toucher, immediately losing all command of themselves, either by an unaccountable sympathy or some other invisible impulse. But as soon as they lasciviously converse together, all that love dies into an envenomed spite. Yet the charmer dares [to] give [the examples of] Elisha's following of Elijah when touched, and [of] Simon and Andrew relinquishing all to follow their true master, for justification of his [charms and] pranks. In this receipt [that is, charm], besides the words [employed], they bestow sometimes a dose composed of spittle and other liquidities [a *glain*], because of its [resemblance to] having an addled egg, similarly intermixed.

There is another charm called *sgiunach* that attracts fishes plentifully to the angler.

But in the more usual charms of curing, besides a general prayer, called the *seachd phaidir* or seventh and perfect prayer [which is] set out below, [and is] composed of some incoherent tautologies, used before and after [the main charming], there are words instituted for transferring of the soul or sickness on [to] other persons, beasts, trees, waters, hills or stones, accordingly as the charmer is pleased to name. The effect [of this] follows wonderfully, which scares many sober persons among the Tramontaines [Highlanders] from going in to see a sick person until they put a dog in before them or [some] one that lives in the house. For where charmers are cherished, they transfer the sickness [by their charms] on to the first living creature that enters [the house] after the charm is pronounced; and such creatures readily rage with pain until they die.

Thus this cheap way of healing distemper without Physic [that is, medicine], does, notwithstanding, pay the account [in] some other way, by sacrificing something to the Original healer, whoever [may] be the [present] instrument [or mediator of healing]. To assess these for the present with the briefs and amulets that make men proof against lead bullets, iron weapons, and the like, I will [next] set down [in writing] some of their more remarkable charms and spells as they are usually written and spoken, one in Latin [and] another in Irish, which I translate. And [I shall also] give the rest, [but] only interpreted, for brevity's sake.

1. The general prayer or Pater Noster, called *Seachd phaidir*, repeated in way of preface and conclusion to every remarkable [that is, individual] charm: Mary is first placed, the Pater Noster of Mary [1], the P.N. or prayer of my King [2], of Mary [3], of the King [4], of Mary [5], of the King [6]. [Then] the Seven Seanings or Salvations to the Son of my King omnipotent.

2. The charm against the palsy and falling sickness [that is, epilepsy] written on paper, and tied about the patient's neck:

In nomine patris et Filii et spiritus sancti, amen. dirupisti Domine vincula mea, tibe sacrificabo Hostiam Laudis sed nomen Domini invocabo, nomen Jesus Nazarenus Rex judeorum, Titulus Triumphalis, Defenda nos ab omnibus malis, Sancte Deus, Sancte Fortis, Sancte et immortalis, miserere nobis + Heloj + Heloj atha + Messias + Σother Immanuel + Pathone + Sabaoth + Tetragammaton + On + Eon + a thonay + alma + avala + Throne + Emmanuel +.

3. The spell to expel the Unbeast.

The order of St Bennet at the appointment of Inachus, to be set about the neck of the infirm, against the sharp-piercing Beast, the unbeast, the White Fistula, the brown cancer, the Flesh cancer, the Bone cancer, come out, thou piercing Worm as my King appointed; either die or flit thy Lodging as Jesus Christ commanded, God and the King omnipotent, either chase you out alive, or slay you within.

These words the Charmer speaks, holding his two thumbs to his mouth, still spitting on them, and then with both thumbs strokes the sore, which daily mends thereafter. They use spitting as an antidote against all that is poisonous and diabolical.

4. A charm [is] spoke[n] in[to] a napkin, and [then] the napkin is sent many miles off, to be tied about a child's open-head to lift it up, as they speak [the charm], and it does the fact [that is, does work].

I will lift up thy bones as Mary lifted up her hands, as the Forks are lifted under the Heavens, as the priest lifts up the upright Mass, up to the crown of thy head I lift thy cheek-bones, the bones of thy hind-head, thy Brow before and behind.

This they labour to justify as to its institution and operation by the reports they hear of the weapon-salve and sympathetic powders, which they suppose may have some such words accompanying [them], and aiding the Natural and sympathetic application. [Such words are believed to] aid the natural and sympathetic application, which may derive from Special Favour of Heaven granted to the first inventor, or from natural properties secretly conveyed, or from some odd invisible physician [as the actors command] that so swiftly carries away [illness] and applies the cure.

5. A spell said to cure a swollen milt [in cattle or sheep].

The skill against a swollen milt, to assuage its wrath, against the sharp milt, the rough milt, the bare milt, the brow milt, against the sharp snouted grey worm that holes and eats the sinews of your heart and vitals.

But now the most dangerous part of this enchantment succeeds [that is, follows], which is the assigning [of] a place for the evil [to go] when expelled. For [in the Bible] the devils, say the charmers, when put out of [a] man, sought [to go] unto the swine; therefore the enchanter proceeds thus when he thinks meet [that is, necessary or fitting]:

He that gives warmth and prosperity, turn from the all hill-envy, or fairy-envy, all Woman-malice, my own malice with them; as the Wind turns about the hillock, Thy Evil Turn from Thee (O Alexander or such) a third part on this Man, a third part on that Woman, a Third on Waters, a Third on Woods, a third on the Brown Harts of the Forest, and a third on the grey stones.

6. There are spells also against bruises, swollen cheeks called the *gollghalar*, the *tarri* or flux, toothache, being smitten with an infectious evil eye, as they call it. There are knots with words tied by a concubine on her paramour's hair that will keep him from carnality with any other during [a period of] her pleasure (an approved cure to it). The same knot is often cast on a thread by sportful [that is, mischievous] people when a party is a-marrying and in front of the Minister. This ties up the man from all benevolence to his bride till the knots be loosed, unless the charm is prevented from making effect by first saluting of the bride after the marriage is consummated [that is, solemnised] and before they leave the Church-yard and dedicated ground.

But what is as strange as any [yet described] [is that] some charmers will extract a mote (particle or growth) out of a person's eye at many mile distance, only the [charmer] must first, spaniel-like, see and smell at something worn by the patient. The words which the charmer utters I have not attained, but his manner is [as follows]: to fill his mouth with water, laying his hands on it. When he has muttered the spell to himself, he pours the water out of his mouth into a very clean vessel, and lets [you] see that very mote in it which molested the person's sight that he was informed of, and who will be found free of it from the time of this action.

Whether [or not] there be a secret reason that a charm has not so much efficacy when uttered by a woman as when by a man, or if because it was first devised by a man, continuing its vigour in the way that it first began, is not worth the time [taken to] dispute it.

These then are the exorcism used for casting out diseases and pains, as heretofore [that is, at one time] they were, to cast out devils, whereof I have given a smattering to let [you] see the many foolish conceits and dangerous customs, in the critical and peremptory observance whereof, many of the Scottish-Irish weary and burden themselves [with], to the greatest neglect of better usages and injunctions.

They set about few actions all the year over without some charm or superstitious rite interwoven [with them], which has no visible natural connection with the affair [in hand], about which it is made, [or] to further it. Yet they have been taught in this manner of old [that is, by tradition] to keep them in an implicit obedience, still busy, and yet still ignorant. Every Age transmits such supposedly profitable folly, and reckons it a greater piaculum to neglect such [traditions] than to transgress God's most holy and undoubted commandments.

This is the secret charm of the Stewarts of Appin, [used] against falling evil [epilepsy] and palsy, [and] tied about the person's neck:

In nomine patris and filij et spiritus sancti Amen. Dirupisti domine vincula mea tibi sacrificabo hostiam laudis, et nomen domini invocabo nomen Jesus Nazarenus Rex judeorum titulus triumphalis Defendas nos ab omnis malis Sancte Deus, Sancte fortis, Sancte et immortalis misere nobis + hieloi + hieloi +

hiloy atonatha + messias + Σother + immanuel + pathone +
Saboath + Tetragammaton + on + eon + a thoney + alma +
avala + throne + emanual +

Telesms, charms and superstition are much of one kind: for
Talismans pretend to be influenced by a constellation through
a mutual and moral relation made between [the parts or
parties] by a Compact, or by a Seasonable dedication. Charms
plead a traditional virtue to [their] words merely upon account
of the prodigious stupendous piety and miraculous power of
the first institutors [thereof].

Superstition, idolatry, [both] presume that Deities inform
ensoul and possess Temples and Images, and that therefore
they become adorable.

The invention of letters was a singular curiosity, now though,
[it is commonplace]. Printing, gunnery, saddles with stirrups,
and several other arts contrivances devices and sciences were
found out after our Saviour's death, and [were] both understood and foreseen by him, yet [he] himself would [not] be
author of either, because albeit they are instruments of good,
they have as direct a tendency to do evil.

The cure of the King's Evil is partly miraculous, partly
complexional, and is much advanced by the piety and health
diet of the Bestower or Receiver; somewhat also by the
apprehension. It is likely to have been first found out [just]
as the nature of many precious stones and minerals, or as
printing and guns, either by Revelation of an Angel, to let
[us] see that God can cure diseases incurable by man, or by
some unexpected accident of person trying conclusions and
conjecturing events. For surely, if we [but] knew them, the
wide Creator has framed many things so, that there are more
ways to save than to destroy.

There is some resemblance also, and allusions in Nature,
that all things being Sevenfold, or composed of it, most usually
have a virtue beyond whatever is composed of any other
number. Examples are such as Sunday, the seventh day of
rest, or the Sun, the seventh planet; Seven being composed of
Four and Three, the Elements and the Trinity, comprehending
both Worlds. But how things having this numeral relation and

resemblance, being so remote, come to partake and derive a Secret Virtue beyond other things from the prototype or first pattern cannot be well given account of. Yet in Ep. Jude, Enoch is named the Seventh (Son) of Adam.

Finis coronat opus.

Written [that is, copied] by Robert Campbell at Inshalladine in the parish of Aberfoyle in Monteith.

Love and Live   1691.

COMMENTARY
ON ASPECTS OF
THE TEXT

Page 21 *These siths [people of the Sidhe] . . . are said to be of a middle nature [halfway] betwixt man and Angel, as were daemons thought to be of old* (see Figure 1). With his opening words Kirk draws a comparison which he develops throughout the remainder of the text: the Fairy people are a specific race or order of life, halfway between humankind and angels. The similarity between this subterranean people and *daemones* is clearly defined, and reinforced by his description which follows (see pages 22–3). Throughout *The Secret Commonwealth* Kirk makes a distinction between fairies or subterraneans which have many similar attributes to *daemones* or advisory entities, and devils or demons, which are historically a later concept within developing Christianity.

At various stages in his exposition he suggests (page 57) that the nature of an Otherworld or fairy contact is defined by the inner condition of the seer: evil or corrupt actions and thoughts will drive away a beneficial advisory entity or companion; conversely, evil, lustful or negative thoughts and emotions will attract vicious or malicious entities.

The original *daemones* in the classical Greek, Roman, and indeed in the early Christian and medieval sense, were held to be neutral in their potential to do good or evil. Some seemed, indeed, to be of an anti-human disposition, while at other times they seemed to be distinctly pro-human. There is, perhaps, a subtle insight below the surface of this discussion of fairies or *daemones* and their potential for good or evil: they tend to respond according to our own personal inner condition.

This concept is found also in the subject of the Co-walker or fairy companion or phantom ally, for these beings, employed widely in magical or sorcerous techniques worldwide, are frequently described as being potentially deadly and dangerous, yet helpful and of great benefit if correctly contacted. Traditional methods of establishing relationships range from the highly ethical and spiritual techniques connected to formal religion, to debased sacrificial practices. Once again, the debased practices lead to dangerous allies, while the ethical or spiritual ones lead to beneficial allies, though no less potentially dangerous.

Kirk deals in various places with this reflex quality or polarised mirroring between human and fairy beings, so we shall return to it later.

The realm of fairy in folklore actually holds a range of beings directly comparable to the range found in pagan religion, from early Celtic sources, to examples in classical and medieval cosmology and spiritual description. The Celtic deities are mainly preserved in early literature, and in some Romano-Celtic evidence from archaeology: their relationship to one another is defined by various interconnected worlds and by the concept of sacred space, sacred directions, and cyclical marriages.[12] Some of these typically Celtic sets of relationships arise in Kirk's treatise, and will be examined as we progress. There is not, however, a hard and fast pantheon of Celtic gods and goddesses that might give us a framework within which to examine fairy lore broadly; this lack is partly due to censorship by orthodox religion expunging the old deities, and partly due to the fluid nature of the Celtic relationship to nature and subtle orders of reality.

While folklorists have frequently commented upon the unclear boundaries between the fairies, ghosts, ancient gods, ancestors, and other entities in collective memory and tradition, a key to this set of relationships may be found, providing we do not apply it too literally or dogmatically, in the classical and post-classical orders of entities, spirits, heroes, daemons, and so forth. These are described in a number of sources, and as Kirk had a concept of this sort in mind as he wrote, it is worth quoting a typical example of the many that might be considered.

In *De Mysteriis Egyptorum*, the work of Iamblichus written in the fourth century AD, we find a very precise description of the orders of supernatural beings. (This text, incidentally, translated and published in 1547 in Europe, seems to have influenced the prophetic development of Nostradamus, as his own techniques of attaining vision are drawn, in part, from Iamblichus.)

In relatively modern magical or esoteric arts the orders or hierarchies of supernatural beings are frequently called 'inner-world' beings, which tends to imply, quite falsely, that they are merely constructions of the imagination. In collective tradition there is no doubt whatsoever as to the reality of the entities, and in Kirk's text their reality is repeatedly affirmed and described in detail, particularly in the context of their physical nature, which he compares in several places to the physical nature of humanity, describing the degrees of difference and the effects that such differences have on fairy and human behaviour.

In most ancient cultures, and indeed in many ethnic magical and religious practices today, many of the levels or types of entity described in the following passage from Iamblichus appear, though the names, of course, vary from culture to culture, and the definition must always be by function. Functional definition is very important in magical divinatory and prophetic events or arts, and one of the great deluding aspects of such arts is the tendency for students to become entirely enmeshed in names and categories, without ever finding the true functions of the beings that they seek to contact.

This functional aspect was clearly grasped by Kirk, as he often cites varied names in English and Gaelic, and qualifies these by describing the activity of the type of entity that he is writing about. He also makes a number of broad categorisations or definitions of entities that behave in certain ways, discriminating, for example, between actual ghosts or spirits of the dead, and simulacra or images of human beings which are sent by fairy communicants to seers (see pages 24, 28 and 31).

In Iamblichus' *De Mysteriis* (ii.4) we find a comprehensive description of the Otherworldly beings, which fits well with divinatory and invocatory practices from the most ancient times to the present day. The author is discussing *epiphanies*, the appearance of supernatural beings, a subject which also appears extensively in Celtic tradition preserved in early literature from Wales and Ireland, though generally in a less formalised presentation, due to the influence of dominant Christianity.

> ... in the case of *gods and goddesses* they sometimes cover the whole sky and the sun and the moon, whilst the earth can no longer remain steady when they descend. When *archangels* appear, certain portions of the world are agitated, and their arrival is heralded by a divided light. The archangels differ in magnitude according to the size of the provinces over which they rule. *Angels* are distinguished by smaller size, and by their being divided numerically. In the case of *daemones* the division goes further, and their magnitude visibly fluctuate. *Heroes* are of a smaller appearance, but of a greater majesty of bearing. Of the *archons* the most powerful belonging to the outer region of the cosmos are large and massive in appearance. Those, on the other hand, who undergo division in the region of matter are apt be to be boastful and generate illusions. *Souls* are not equal in size, but are generally smaller in appearance than heroes.
>
> Next let us define the distinctions between the appearances of these beings who make themselves manifest. In the case of gods who make themselves manifest, what is seen is clearer than truth itself; every detail shines out exactly and its articulations are shown in brilliant light. The appearances of archangels are still true and full. Those of angels maintain the same character, but their being is not expressed in the image seen with the same fullness [as that of archangels]. Those of daemones are blurred, and even more blurred are those of heroes. In the case of archons those who are cosmic powers are clearly perceived, but those who are involved in matter are blurred. Yet both give an impression of power, whereas the appearance of souls is merely shadowy.

We shall examine later (Appendix 7) the descriptions of *daemones* and orders or hierarchies of entities found in the works of Geoffrey of Monmouth (twelfth century), some of which Kirk certainly had read, and which he cites in connection with Merlin. There is no implication that Kirk borrowed from classical or other early authors, but that such authors, including Kirk himself and many later writers, borrowed from perennial traditions, preserved both . orally and in written form.

Page 21 [*They are of*] *light changeable bodies, like those called Astral, somewhat of the nature of a condensed cloud, and best seen in twilight.* In this passage Kirk affirms the physical nature of the Fairies: he always treats of them as entities of higher or more active subtle forms of matter, but physical nevertheless. This is a deep-rooted tradition, and just as the fairies are able to influence or appear in the human world, so may human beings step into, or be carried off into, the fairy realm, which is subterranean. Throughout *The Secret Commonwealth* we need to bear in mind that Kirk and his Gaelic countrymen, some even to this day, always regard the fairies as physical entities.

After describing the method of nourishment, which consists of draining various fluids and vital energies from foodstuffs without actually consuming the main body of the food itself (once again presented as proof of physical but subtly higher bodies), Kirk touches upon the subject of fairy helpers:

Page 22 *Some [of them] were old before the Gospel dispelled paganism, and in some Barbarous places as yet, [they] enter houses . . . [to] set the kitchens in order . . . Such drudges go under the name of Brounies.* This is a widespread, often confused, but persistent belief, that has caused many comments from folklorists: country people believe that physical entities, albeit from the fairy realm, clean their houses for them. They leave food out for these fairies, which food is not touched thereafter by humans, for its essence has been drained to feed the fairy helper. The belief in the fairy helpers, among people of all ages, is literal, though the sceptical commentator might ask where is the daily evidence of their beneficial work around the house?

Kirk describes the Brownies, the lowest or humblest fairy ally first: he may be deliberately scaling his descriptions, for the higher forms of the Co-walker and prophetic ally are described later in the text. The concept of interaction and polarity or mirroring, which is central to fairy and underworld traditions, is introduced immediately in this, at first humble, context (page 22): *When we have plenty, they have scarcity at their homes . . .* In terms of mythology and folklore we have two possible sources of derivation for these lower orders of fairy described by Kirk: the first is that of the range or hierarchy of fairy entities and helpers, of which he gives further examples in more exalted circumstances. A parallel is found in the simple household gods of pagan cultures: small shrines and offerings were kept in Roman households, for example, to very basic deities. These were at the 'lower' end of the scale of divinities, just as the Brownies are at the lower end of the scale of fairy beings.

Page 22 *Their bodies of congealed air are sometimes carried aloft, while [at] others [they] grovel in different shapes, and enter into any cranny or cleft of the Earth where air enters, [as if] to their ordinary dwellings. The Earth being full of cavities and cells, and there being no place or creature but is supposed to have other animals, greater or lesser, living in, or upon it, as inhabitants . . . [there is] no such thing as pure wilderness in the whole Universe.* This passage is part of Kirk's main argument of interconnecting and interacting entities: today we would say that he regards the Universe as a holism. Indeed, the concept is one well established at two extremes, that of mysticism and that of the most recent developments in modern science. This holistic world-view is repeated elsewhere (page 26), and Kirk affirms at one point that it was one of the beliefs taught among the seers themselves. If we grant that Kirk is reporting accurately, then he is not making a philosophical thesis of his own, but reporting the remnants of an esoteric or mystical tradition, preserved from the days of pagan Celtic religion and philosophy.

This undertone of a perennial wisdom-teaching runs throughout Celtic tradition, but it is intermingled with a vast range of humble beliefs, superstitions, and variants of orthodox religion. It is interesting to consider, from Kirk's evidence, that a certain amount of philosophical instruction was handed down among seers, over and above the initiatory and interpretative lore that is well recorded.

Pages 22–3 They remove to other lodgings at the beginning of each Quarter of the year, so traversing until doomsday . . . And at such revolutions of time, Seers or men of the second sight . . . have very terrifying encounters with them . . . Therefore . . . [they] have made it a custom . . . to keep Church duly every first Sunday of the Quarter . . . And . . . will not be seen again in Church till the next Quarter [day] begins . . . The Quarters or Seasons (see Figure 2) are the turning points of both the pagan and the Christian Wheel of the Year. The four great nodes or turnings were celebrated at approximately the spring and autumn equinox and the summer and winter

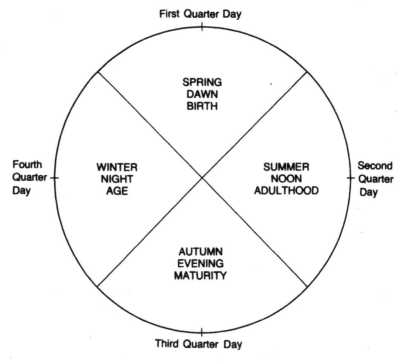

Figure 2. The Wheel of Life (the Four Seasons)

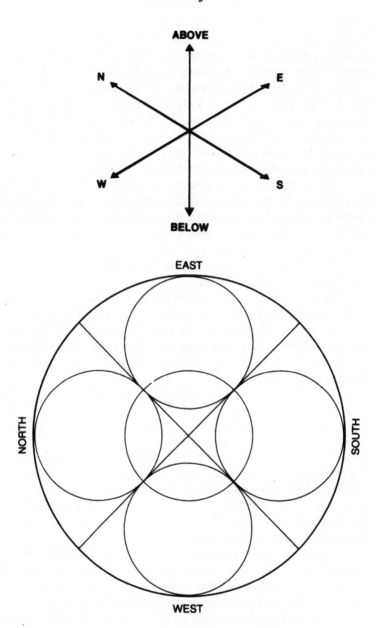

Figure 3. The Sacred Directions and Zones

solstice, though these events were also governed by other criteria. The Celtic festivals, though often said to be defined by the solar phases of the year, were also marked by the rising and setting of the Pleiades, celebrated in May and November.

There are several implications in this tradition of the fairy people travelling to 'other lodgings' at each Quarter or the turning point of each Season. As this concept of revolution and cycles occurs again in Kirk's text, and is fundamental to much of underworld and fairy tradition, we may briefly consider some of these implications at this early stage.

1. The fairies are connected to the vitality of the land; thus they are similar to, but not in all cases identical with, pagan entities such as nature spirits, *genii loci*, and deities related to certain locations and ancient sites. (Kirk touches upon this comparison on pages 49 and 54). Thus when the Seasons turn, they themselves move accordingly around the Wheel of the Year or the Wheel of Life.

2. They travel so until doomsday: this carries within it some further implications and connections, the most obvious being that the fairies are pagan, unhallowed entities, and therefore cannot find rest. But as is often the case with tradition, there are deeper levels to this concept, reaching beyond that of mere religious propaganda.

(a) The fairies are often identified with wandering troops of earth-bound spirits, though Kirk makes some very clear distinctions between fairies and the spirits of the dead (pages 24 and 30) and there seems little doubt that he was drawing these distinctions from tradition rather than rationalising for the purposes of his text. In pagan religion, such as that of both the Scandinavians and the Celts, the souls of the dead are gathered up by the Wild Hunt in November (coinciding with the appearance of the Pleiades), now celebrated as Hallowe'en, and known in Gaelic as *Samhain*.

(b) Early Celtic traditions are of a semi-nomadic people (though we should be cautious in making generalisations): the ancient land of Ireland, for example, was divided geomantically into Five Zones [13] consisting of Four Quarters according to the Sacred Four Directions (see Figure 3) with a fifth central zone. Each zone had its magical, social, and professional or caste divisions. The court of the High King, however, travelled around the idealised land (wherever it might be, Ireland being merely one historical example preserved in early literature and tradition) from zone to zone. This concept of a sacred land divided into Directions and Zones has been widely studied by scholars of Indo-European tradition [14] and has its counterpart worldwide.

(c)On its deepest level it is a mirror or reflex image of the ancient concept of the Wheel of Life, around which all creatures travel until they are freed of incarnation. As reincarnation is specifically described by Kirk as one of the beliefs held by the seers (page 26) we may touch upon this aspect of wisdom-tradition which is found in many world religions, though it was eventually erased from Christianity, remaining as an underground tradition only.

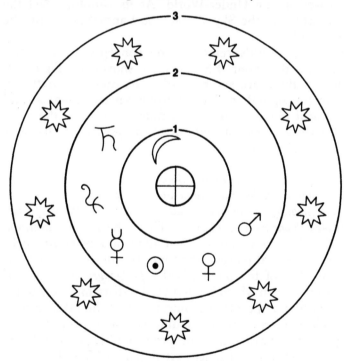

Figure 4. The Three Worlds, Stars, and Planets

Page 23 *They are . . . seen . . . to eat at funerals, banquets . . . to carry the bier or coffin with the corpse, among the Middle-Earth men to the grave.* The fairies are frequently associated with death and events surrounding death, though Kirk takes pains to separate the fairies, with their own orders and tribes and *polity* (page 28) and the spirits or departed souls of dead humans. The use of the phrase Middle-Earth is worth noting, both in its use by Kirk and its preservations in Scottish-English dialect and early English. In Norse and Scandinavian mythology[15] the term is used for the Middle World, that of humans. The concept is rooted in a primal magical cosmology of Three Worlds: Over-World, Middle-World and Under-World. Humans dwell in the Middle-World, certain gods and goddesses, angels, and divine messengers or spirits in the Over-World, while other deities, fairies and ancestral spirits dwell in the Under-World. At its simplest level the Three Worlds are the Sky-World, the Land-World, and the Under-World.

The Three Worlds relate to the concepts of stars and planets and the Four Elements as shown in Figure 4, and though there are several variations upon the patterns, the basic conceptual model underpins ancient magical and metaphysical thought from the simplest models to the more refined, such as those of Plato or of the Jewish or Hermetic Neoplatonic Kabbalah.

Page 23 *Some men of that exalted Sight . . . have seen . . . a double-man . . . that is, a Superterranean and a Subterranean Inhabitant perfectly resembling one another in all points, whom [the seer] could . . . distinguish one from the other . . .* This is Kirk's first mention of the double, reflex man or Co-walker, a subject which he discusses in several places. Although the subject seems to be similar to that of the popularised *doppelganger* or *astral body* (*astral* being a term which is often used indiscriminately today but which had a specific meaning to Kirk), he takes care to inform his readers that the double is not a 'projection' or 'thought-form'. This concept of 'projection' is possibly found in some of the other instances cited (pages 38 and 44), but as a rule Kirk always refers to a reflex or fairy being that mirrors the mortal, rather than an energy, image, or efflux from the human being.

Page 23 [*The Seers*] *avouch that every Element and different state of being has [in it] Animals resembling those of another Element . . . So as the Roman [Catholic] invention of good and bad daemons and guardian Angels . . . is called by [the Seers] an ignorant mistake [deriving] . . . from this original [resemblance or reflection] of species through the Elements.* Kirk uses this paragraph to mock the Catholic Church gently, and employs the frequently cited instance of the 'monk-fish', which was known persistently, along with other examples of mimicry, from medieval literature onwards. Although we do not subscribe to these crude examples as proof, the concept of Elemental-reflection of entities, and of morphology or morphic resonance, has gained a new scientific stature in recent years.[16] The suggestion that the Gaelic seers ascribed the orthodox religious definition of good and bad demons or angels to a misunderstanding of the perennial metaphysics of reflection and polarity is rather a startling one, for this same concept is taught in esoteric traditions, in which the crude notion of opposites is transcended through the understanding of harmonics, reflections, and relative modes of being. One simple approach to this relationship between beings and worlds in traditional meta-physics is shown in Figure 1.

Page 24 *They call this Reflex-man a* coimimeadh *or Co-walker, every way like the man, as a Twin-brother and Companion . . . both before and after the Original [man] is dead. And [this Co-walker] was . . . often seen . . . to enter a house; by which the people knew that the person [himself] . . . was to visit them within a few days. This copy, Echo, or living picture, goes at last to his own herd. It accompanied that [living] person . . . for ends best known to itself, whether to guard him from the secret assaults . . . or only . . . to counterfeit all his actions.* The Co-walker is now defined further, making it clear that this is not a projection from the human, but a fairy being that mimics a mortal, sometimes to protect him from assaults of other entities, sometimes in mockery.

Page 24 *If invited and earnestly required, these companions make themselves known and familiar to men, otherwise, being in a different state and Element, they neither can nor will easily converse with them.* This sentence is derived from the long-enduring tradition of contact between the Worlds, which seems always to be dependent upon the initiation or adjustment of perception in humanity. Kirk asserts elsewhere that though the subterranean people can see us, we cannot easily see them (pages 47–8). Conversation or direct contact with your Co-walker is one of the chthonic magical techniques, found in underworld or shamanistic initiation worldwide. It has its mirror or reflex in the technique of *Conversation with the Holy Guardian Angel*, found in Kabbalistic and Christian mysticism, and featured in esoteric ritual and contemplative training.

Page 24 . . . *these Subterraneans eat but little in their dwellings, their food being exactly clean, and served up by pleasant children like enchanted puppets. What food they extract from us is conveyed to their homes by secret paths* . . . The subtle nature of the fairies and their means of nourishment are further discussed, combined with some folklore on drawing milk away by magic, as practised not by the fairies but by *skilful women*, or witches. The image of the pleasant children like enchanted puppets belongs to the exotic scenario which follows:

Page 25 *Their houses are called large and fair . . . unperceivable by vulgar eyes, like Rachland and other Enchanted Islands; having for light continual lamps, and fires, often seen [burning] without fuel to sustain them.* This description is a variant of one that has been repeated in different forms in a number of literary sources that might have been available to Kirk, but also has its place repeatedly in oral tradition. It seems to derive from fusion of pagan myths of the Otherworld with collective memory of actual ritual practices, many of which are confirmed by archaeology. The mythic element is the most important, as the historical ritual element derives from it.

(a) The Otherworld, in Kirk's treatise, is subterranean, but he compares it with mythical or enchanted islands. Such islands were part of the Celtic legendary tradition, and both the subterranean and marine Otherworlds were places of beauty, timelessness, light, and power. To the

modern imagination, a realm beneath the earth suggests
cold rock, damp, darkness, fear, and perhaps burning fire
and punishment, deriving from the long centuries of religious
propaganda concerning Hell. But in earlier tradition the
underworld was said to be a place filled with light, with
many realms or great dimensional realms and spaces. It is
in this kind of location that the fairy houses in Kirk's text are
located.

We find a detailed psychopompic or initiatory journey
through the underworld in the Ballad and the Romance
Poem of Thomas Rhymer, deriving from a thirteenth-century
historical poet, who uttered many local prophecies, some
of which seem to have come true.[17] In Thomas's vision, the
underworld or Elfland contains rivers of blood and water, vast
plains, a magical Tree of Life, and beautiful halls. It is lit not
by the sun or moon, but by a supernatural light, or in some
versions by the light of the stars shining within the earth.

(b) Perpetual fires or lamps, a subject which Kirk returns to
later (page 37), and from which he derives the term *lychnobious
people* to describe the fairies (see Kirk's own Glossary beginning
on page 165), were kept burning in ancient temples. The
great example in Celtic culture was the perpetual fire at
the sanctuary of St Brigit in Kildare in Ireland. This Saint
narrowly disguises the Celtic goddesses Brigh or Brigid, to
whom many hundreds of Gaelic prayers were uttered. There is
some evidence that the early Christian church at Glastonbury
was based on a pagan temple of Brigid, and many other
examples of her presence in Britain and Ireland could be
cited.

The original goddess mediated the energies of poetry and
inspiration, smithcraft, and therapy. In Celtic Christian tradition she was midwife to Mary and/or foster mother to Jesus.
We may see echoes of this in the many examples of the theme of
the Otherworld or fairy child and the human nurse or midwife,
though this comparison need not be extended too far.

A perpetual fire was kept burning in the Temple of Vesta in
Rome, and in the ancient Egyptian Temple of Neith in Saïs. In
Britain the ancient Temple of Sulis Minerva had a perpetual
fire, which was recorded in the legendary *History of the Kings*

of Britain by Geoffrey of Monmouth, a text with which Kirk was undoubtedly familiar. In Geoffrey's *Vita Merlini* we find a detailed description of the Otherworld Island, known as the Fortunate Isle, and ruled over by a mysterious priestess or goddess of flight, shape-changing and therapy, with her sisters. Curiously, if we follow Geoffrey's text,[18] the Fortunate Isle seems to be reached by entering the earth through the sacred springs guarded by King Bladud, the Celtic god-king presiding over the site of Aquae Sulis.[19]

Geoffrey of Monmouth also gives a detailed set of Prophecies uttered by Merlin,[20] and describes in detail the youthful Merlin, born of a daemon and a mortal woman (something to which Kirk refers on page 62), bursting into tears before making his prophetic utterances. This crying, blinking, twinkling of the eye, is a well-attested feature of the Second Sight.

Page 25 *Women are yet alive who tell they were taken away when in child-bed to nurse ffayrie children, a lingering voracious image of [themselves] being left in their place* . . . The mortal nurse for fairy children is a widespread theme, and one which Kirk returns to in some detail later, citing a specific case contemporary to himself. The false human, a substitution also associated traditionally with that of children stolen away into fairyland, eventually expires: in Kirk's later, more detailed, example a wife returns from the fairy realm and is reunited with her husband. One again the emphasis is upon a physical translation into the subterranean dimension:

Page 25 . . . *she neither perceives any passage out, nor sees what these people do in other rooms of the Lodging. When the [fairy] child is weaned, the nurse either dies, or is conveyed back, or gets to choose to stay there.* The three choices are resonant of triple patterns in a number of legends: in Thomas Rhymer's vision, the Queen of Elfland shows him three roads, that of Righteousness leading to Heaven, the road of Wickedness taken by mortals, and the road to Elfland, upon which they travel onwards to her mysterious hall or palace. It is interesting that Kirk states precisely that the mortal nurse may be offered the choice of staying in the subterranean realm.

If we consider this triplication in an initiatory context, the three choices – death, return to the human world, or remaining in the realm of fairy – are very close to those visionary roads shown to Thomas. In bardic initiations the candidate spent a night in a sacred site, after which he was either dead, mad, or a poet. Similar transits or thresholds at sacred sites are found in religious and magical arts worldwide, in which candidates sit in graveyards, in caves, or at crossroads.

In the context of the fairy nurse, Kirk next describes (page 25) the motif in which a human, gaining sight of the fairies through magical means, may be stricken blind with a puff of their breath. This is found in a large number of folk tales in variant forms, as is the belief that the fairies abhor iron, which is described in the following paragraph. There is a striking similarity between the traditional explanation of the fairies' dislike for iron, and the cosmology and bardic topography or holistic world-view found restated in the *Vita Merlini*: (Appendix 7).

Page 26 *Their apparel and speech is like that of the people and country under which they live . . . They speak but little, and that by way of whistling, clear, not rough. The very devils conjured in any country do answer in the language of that place, yet sometimes these subterraneans do speak more distinctly than at other times.* Many examples of fairy lore show them wearing the costume of past ages, but Kirk explicitly states that they wear the contemporary costume of the region in which they live. He also makes a firm identification between the fairies and the land, something to which he returns on several occasions, and extends this concept to evil spirits or devils, stating that both they and the fairies can talk in the speech of the region in which they are contacted. These passages are rooted in the extremely ancient pagan religion of the Celts, in which the Land and the spirits of the land, including but not limited to ancestral spirits, are unified in the underworld.

Page 26 *They live much longer than we [do], yet die at last, or at least vanish . . . For it is one of their Tenets that nothing perishes, but, as the Sun and [the] Year, everything goes [around] in a Circle, Lesser or*

Greater, and is renewed, and refreshed in its revolutions. As it is another [tenet] that Every Body in the Creation moves, which [movement] is a sort of life, and that nothing moves but what has another Animal moving on it, and so on, to the utmost minute corpuscle that [is] capable to be a receptacle of Life. This remnant of ancient philosophy is far removed from the usual fairy lore, and forms part of the thread of a perennial wisdom-tradition that runs through Kirk's text. The cycle that he describes is the Wheel of Life, with a direct statement of reincarnation or rebirth into various other states after death. The concept of movement as life is tantalisingly modern, even materialist at first superficial glance, but the tenet is really a holistic one, with life forms and energies interpenetrating one another ceaselessly. The microscope was known in Kirk's day (he mentions it on page 34), but this refined concept of multiple life forms within and upon one another has only been developed scientifically in more recent centuries with technological advances. It does, however, have a number of possible correspondences in classical philosophy.

The interrelationship between life forms is found in early Celtic legends involving the season of the year, orders or long lists of totem beasts, and the interaction of the Four Elements. These interactive tales or cycles are found in Irish sagas, in the Welsh *Mabinogion* and in the *Vita Merlini*. We may see them also in the myths of Orpheus (similar in many ways to that of the youthful or mad Merlin or to the search for Mabon in *Khllwch and Olwen* in the *Mabinogion*), or the tragic myth of Balder in Norse legend. In these tales, the interaction of all life is shown through orders of animals and other entities, all of which depend upon a central figure, usually a Divine Son or Child of Light. The cyclical nature of these myths is frequently connected to the Seasons of the year, and there are firm analogies or reflections of the cycles of birth, life, death, and rebirth of the mortal world, but extending into, or rather depending on or reflecting from, other mythic dimensions.

Page 27 They are said to have aristocratic rulers and laws, but no discernible religion ... They disappear whenever they hear ... the name of Jesus, at which all do bow willingly or by constraint that dwell above or beneath [or] within the Earth ... This is the first

of a series of biblical quotations that Kirk uses to prove his
developing case for the physical existence of the fairy people
and their subterranean world. The modern reader needs to
be constantly aware that the Biblical quotations were cited
as firm (almost incontrovertible) evidence, not as comparative
religious theories or mere dogmatic assertions. As a devout
Christian, Kirk would have had no hesitation in proposing
these supportive quotes, though the manner in which he
uses them and the verses which he selects are sometimes
surprising. When we come to his criticism of Lord Tarbett's
letter to Robert Boyle (page 45) we find Kirk marshalling
his scientific, religious, and legal arguments separately, but
confirming one another. Part of the scholarly technique of the
day, stemming from the medieval period and perpetuated as
late as the nineteenth century, was to assemble the natural,
legal and religious evidence for a case side by side, and then
show how they supported and reinforced one another to prove
the main thesis.

Having stated that Biblical quotations were an essential
part of Kirk's evidence, just as essential to his thesis as actual
cases, techniques, and examples from the Gaelic traditions of
seership, we must beware of taking them as mere examples
of the fanatical religion of the time. The first quotation,
from Philipians 2:10, is a good example of the many levels
of meaning found in the Biblical citations that Kirk lists. The
verse refers to the 'Harrowing of Hell', the Christian variant
of a widespread myth in which the Saviour or Sacred One
descends into the underworld to liberate the spirits entrapped
there.

The difference between the pagan traditions and the Christian one is a difference of degree rather than actual content:
the descent of Jesus into the underworld (later dogmatised
as the 'Harrowing of Hell') was a universal ultimate descent,
that subsumed all earlier sacrificial rituals or revelations. Kirk
tells in his later chapters that the seers themselves use Biblical
precedents in training their pupils, and we shall return to
this interplay between Christianity and pagan Gaelic seership
again.

Page 27 *The . . . seer . . . can bring them with a spell to appear to himself or [to] others . . . He tells that they are ever readiest to go on hurtful errands, but seldom will be the messengers of great good to men. He is not terrified . . . when he calls them, but seeing them by surprise . . . frightens him extremely.* Seership can be trained or untrained: this is a subject which Kirk, and Tarbett, and other commentators upon the Second Sight, mention as a feature of its appearance and currency in Gaelic culture. The trained seer, presumably subscribing to the techniques and ancient magical and metaphysical tenets which Kirk cites, controls his Sight with a spell. The spell can cause the fairy people to appear to the seer, or to others (a subject which we shall return to shortly), but when he sees them naturally or unexpectedly, they cause him extreme fright. In other words, a certain amount of training is necessary to control the Sight, and preparation is required even for an experienced seer not to be shocked by random visions of *earnest ghastly staring looks, skirmishes, and the like.*

Kirk describes one of the most basic aspects of the Second Sight, which is that the seer seldom sees anything good, but often sees bad events that will come to pass. This is the meaning of the *hurtful errands,* as compared to messages of *great good.*

This negative aspect of the Sight is affirmed even today by those who have it: it often comes against the seer's will, and usually shows negative events that will come to pass, such as injuries, deaths, disasters, and so forth. We need to exercise the same careful judgement of this as Kirk himself, for he states elsewhere in his text that the fairies may offer these visions to warn men and to lead them to better lives, rather than out of spite. The spiteful element is, however, widespread in folk tradition concerning supernatural beings, so we cannot pretend that all is sweetness and light: the subject is related to the attitude or spiritual or emotional state of the seer, as we have discussed above, and as Kirk discusses on page 57.

Page 27 *They are said to have many pleasant Toyish Books. But the operation of these pieces only appears in some paroxysms of antic Corybantic jollity – as if ravished and prompted by a new spirit entering into them ... Other Books they have of involved abstruse sense, much like the Rosicrucian style.* Two classes of fairy books are described, and in the same paragraph Kirk states that they do not have the Bible as a book of protection against evil, but use collections of charms and counter-charms instead. This last description is resonant of the pre-Christian origin of much fairy lore. The two classes of books, however, are more suggestive of classical lore. The first is a description of prophetic books or divinatory systems, the operation of which only works in a fit or paroxysms, ravished by the entry of a new spirit. Kirk is drawing a comparison to the Delphic oracle, which could only utter obscure verses when the Pythoness was taken over by the spirit of the god Apollo. This comparison is found again on page 36, comparing an old woman of the Second Sight with the Delphian priestess. Kirk leavens the use of antic spirit inspiration (which was of course frowned upon and punishable), by making it a matter of jollity and merriment.

The second class of fairy books are involved and abstruse, much like the Rosicrucian style. Here Kirk is referring to a class of literature that created something of a sensation only a few years before he was writing, and to which additions were published by various authors as late as the eighteenth and nineteenth centuries. There are a number of modern books on the origin of the Rosicrucian movement, but the most thorough analysis was published by Thomas de Quincey (author of *The Confessions of an English Opium Eater*) in 1871. Essentially the Rosicrucians were supposed to be a mysterious order of wise men, versed in mystical, therapeutic and alchemical, or magical, arts. Various allegories and technical instructions were published in their name from the close of the sixteenth century onwards, the most famous being the *Fama Fraternitas of the meritorious order of the Rosy Cross*, an initiatory and visionary text modelled upon the ancient Mysteries, but including many subtle and obscure esoteric Christian elements.

As many of the Rosicrucian or would-be Rosicrucian books contain descriptions and illustrations of the relationship between worlds and orders of being, such as Robert Fludd's works published in England (which Kirk might have had access to), it may be that Kirk is drawing this kind of comparison. He would certainly not be suggesting that the fairies subscribed to a mystical Protestant ethic designed to undermine Catholic supremacy in parts of Europe, which was apparently one of the aims of the early Rosicrucian publications.

But as Caitlin Matthews[21] and a number of other writers have demonstrated, much of the Rosicrucian mythos was based upon Germanic Teutonic and Celtic legends circulating in Europe. The motifs of underground chambers, perpetual lamps, and the theme of a hero who courts a mysterious underworld lover, are all found in various refined literary variants in Rosicrucian publications: the audience of the day would not have found these images exotic or unfamiliar. So when Kirk mentions Rosicrucian texts he is referring to a more or less contemporary literature, with a profound Christian ethic that draws upon ancient mythic emblems and motifs for its imagery and a substantial part of its inspiration. This is not unlike his own humble book, drawing upon Gaelic fairy lore for a thesis proving the Otherworld, and so countering materialism and atheism. A summary of the main Rosicrucian legend, at least as far as it was published, is found in Appendix 1, drawn from De Quincey's *Suspiria De Profundis*.

Page 27 And albeit Were-Wolves and Witches true bodies are . . . wounded at home when the[ir] astral assumed bodies are stricken elsewhere . . . these [fairy] people have not a second . . . body at all to be so pierced. Here Kirk is referring to lore widespread in Europe, which asserts that a witch or werewolf may be discovered at home by wounds appearing on the body, often of a quite respectable and hitherto unsuspected person, resulting from wounds inflicted elsewhere upon their astral double or animal shape. The fairies have only one body, that of lightened, refined, less gross substance, which when assaulted or divided by a blow reunites itself. Kirk again makes the distinction between these subtle bodies of Air, by which he means metaphysical Air rather than gaseous air, and the usual astral double or assumed form that may be taken by humans.

Page 28 *Some men say their continual sadness is because of their*
... unchangeable condition ... But other Men of the second sight
... vary from these [interpretations] ... averring those subterranean
people to be departed souls attending a while in their inferior state,
and clothed with [temporary] bodies procured through their Alms-deeds
... that they may not scatter, nor wander and be lost in the Totum
[plenum or fullness] or [in] their first nothing [the Void]. But if
any ... have given no alms ... they sleep in an inactive state until
they resume Terrestrial Bodies again. Several significant traditions
are reported here, the first being the widespread one of the
fairy sadness at their immortality and being possibly banned
from heaven by an orthodox Deity. This theme, 'the burden
of unimagined time' was pursued by the Scottish poet Fiona
Macleod (William Sharp) in his fairy drama, *The Immortal
Hour*, which was adapted and set to music by Rutland
Boughton[22] in England in the early twentieth century. While
it does play some part in fairy tradition, it stems from poetic
interpretation of Christian dogma.

The concept that the fairies are the spirits of the dead in a
temporary or even permanent condition of subterranean life
is widespread, and in tradition itself we find the ancestors,
the recently dead, the fairies, and the gods, goddesses and
elemental beings, all inhabiting the underworld together,
sometimes jointly and sometimes in separate realms, dimensions, or states within the underworld. The tradition of a
spiritual body being built by generosity or alms-deeds is
found in various forms worldwide, and is by no means
limited to Gaelic or pagan-Christian Celtic belief. In *The
Lyke Wake Dirge*, an English song of reputedly ancient origin,
various post-mortem states are gained successively by donning
clothing and shoes and partaking of food and drink which were
given as alms in the mortal life (See Appendix 2).

The temporary or limbo body, a vehicle gained by compassion, lives in the Fairy Realm, rather than being scattered,
or wandering in the Totum, the fullness of the Universe, or
returning to the first nothing or Void. These are abstruse
metaphysical concepts, perhaps familiar to modern esoteric
students from Kabbalah or Tibetan Buddhism, where the
infinite Universe (Kirk's Totum) is founded upon an utter

Void (Kirk's First Nothing). They do not play a great part
in the orthodox Christianity of the seventeenth century, and
if we grant that Kirk is indeed reporting oral tradition, this
is further evidence of a specific wisdom-teaching of ancient
origins, but with perennial and worldwide currency. Finally
we have the reference to reincarnation: for the souls sleep in an
inactive state until they resume Terrestrial Bodies again. An
unambiguous statement directly counter to Christian dogma.

As Kirk is reporting the beliefs of his barbarian parishioners, presumably he can avoid any suggestion of heresy
or witchcraft, but we need to remember constantly that
seventeenth-century Scotland, and indeed England, had recently emerged from the fanatical conflict of the Revolution,
based on extreme Protestantism and religious prejudice. Of
course it need hardly be added that the type of lore that
Kirk describes was strictly banned by all Christian sects
and authorities, Catholic, Protestant, and multiple orthodox
or unorthodox variants thereof.

Kirk next reports a typical death and sickness tradition
(page 28) in which the wraith or death-dog appears, but he
gives it an interesting interpretation, saying that this wraith is
the *exuded fumes of the man approaching death* and, like astral bodies
tossed in the wind, it is neither a true soul nor a counterfeiting
spirit.

Page 28 *Yet not a few vouch . . . that surely these are a numerous
people by themselves, having their own polities.* Having stated
this, which is his own viewpoint as well as one asserted in
tradition, Kirk then reminds us, quite correctly, that there
are inconsistencies in tradition, due to diversity of judgements.
Today we would say due to diversity in the streams or strands
of the collective memory.

Page 29 *Their weapons are . . . a Stone . . . shaped like a Barbed
arrow head, but flung as a dart with great force . . . subtly and mortally
wounding the vital parts . . . Some of these wounds I have . . . felt
. . . with my [own] hands.* The elf-bolt is a mysterious weapon
that strikes without breaking the skin, but wounds terribly and
subtly: neolithic flint arrowheads and other tools were often

thought to be inactive or spent fairy weapons. This instance and several others scattered throughout the text, plus Kirk's own interest in the therapeutic powers of seventh children may lead us to the conclusion that he had, or was believed by his parishioners to have, healing skills. Kirk was himself a seventh son, and tells us that merely by laying finger upon a fairy wound it may be cured, that he has felt fairy wounds, and so forth.

By comparison we may consider that the Rev. Sabine Baring-Gould, another clergyman deeply involved in pagan lore, but living in Devon in the early twentieth century, reported active traditions of White Witches (his own words) and healers. Some of the spells that Baring-Gould noted are similar in style and content to those described by Kirk towards the close of his treatise (see Appendix 5). In *Devon Notes and Queries*, October 1906, a writer stated that local people came to his door to ask for the healing touch of the seventh daughter of his family, who was then only a baby.

Page 29 *The men of that Second Sight do not [simply] discover strange things when asked, but . . . [in] fits and Raptures . . .* This is repeatedly asserted, that the Sight comes as a sudden fit and not as a steady faculty: a seer recounted to Kirk that he fought off the fit by out-wrestling or by cutting a fairy communicant in two with an iron weapon, upon which the fairy vanished. Most seers are not of such sturdy stuff.

Page 29 *. . . neighbours often perceived this man to disappear . . . and . . . about one hour after to become visible [again] . . . nearly a bow-shot from the first place . . . where . . . those subterraneans did . . . combat with him.* This is the first description of a physical transportation or translation witnessed by others, unlike that of the nurse described earlier (page 25): the typical pattern is that someone vanishes physically for a short period of time, reappearing at some distance from his or her original location. Kirk cites several other instances of this, and is himself connected with a local tradition in Aberfoyle that he did not die, but was translated into the underworld or fairy realm.

Page 30 *As Birds and Beasts . . . foresee storms, so those invisible people . . . understand, by [using] the Book of Nature, things [yet] to come . . .* The theory of fairy beings, with subtle bodies, is further developed by analogy to the natural abilities of certain birds and animals. The analogy and educational use of bird and animal examples is often found in living wisdom-traditions: nowadays we often call this system one of 'totem beasts' drawing on a term from native American tradition, but it is clear from a mass of evidence that it was highly developed by the pagan Celts. Much of Celtic myth and legend, including early Irish texts, the Welsh *Mabinogion*, and many of the Grail legends, involves transformation through the action of or interaction with magical animals. It seems very likely that the use of bird and animal analogies in explaining the action of the Second Sight was something that Kirk encountered in Gaelic tradition, along with the examples discussed earlier (page 26) in which all life-forms interact and holistically resonate within one another.

Kirk returns to this theory several times, and it is part of his scientific exposition and development of his thesis. The process that Kirk defines is as follows:

1. The fairy people can, through *natural* means, but of a subtlety unavailable to man, have foreknowledge of events, just as a bird or animal can scent or see subtle hints of distant humans.

2. The seers are able to perceive the fairy people, who in turn convey messages to them by symbolic actions or shows. Sometimes the seer has a fairy companion or Co-walker.

3. There are obscure, diffuse, but ample, traditions of interpretation and apparently ancient pagan philosophy attached to this relationship between humans and fairies. These initiatory traditions are formally separated (as Kirk himself affirms) in training by certain seers, though usually they are freely mixed with general folklore of all sorts.

Page 30 *. . . a man of the Second Sight perceiving the operations of these forecasting invisible people . . . indulged through a stupendous providence to give warnings of . . . remarkable events, either in the Air, Earth, or Waters . . .* The method is again defined, and linked to the Elemental Fourfold model (see Figure 8). At the close of his book Kirk gives a typical esoteric Elemental theory for the power of seventh children, as it arises (he says) from the fusion of the Four Elements with the spiritual power of the Trinity (see page 70 and Figure 8).

Page 30 . . . *he saw a . . . shroud creep up around a walking healthy person's legs* . . . This is a classic example of Second Sight, and as the shroud progresses so does the person draw nearer to death. It must be stressed that this is, in Kirk's thesis, a symbolic action made by the fairy people, and not an efflux from the human, nor is it an example of 'clairvoyance' or perception of the human aura. The fairy tradition is a very specific one of contact between human and underworld or Otherworldly entities, with its own techniques and symbolic language.

Page 31 *There be many places called Fairy Hills, which the mountain people think impious and dangerous to . . . uncover . . . believing the souls of their predecessors to dwell therein. And to that end, they say, a Mote or Mount was dedicated beside every Church-yard, to receive the souls until their adjacent bodies arise, and so becomes as a Fairy-hill* . . . Fairy hills are either natural locations, or ancient ritual or burial structures. On occasions we find the two functions combined. A proportion of this belief, that the ancestors dwell in the fairy hills, stems from prehistoric cultures, first because the ancestors' bodies are literally in the fairy mounds, but second, and on a deeper level of belief, because the forces of life, death and regeneration were inherent within the underworld. Celtic, pagan religion was a complex fusion of ancestral and nature lore, with very fluid images of gods and goddesses connected, like the ancestors, to a Sacred Land. Much of this was preserved in folk tradition, becoming modified by Christianity until beliefs such as that concerning the church-yard mound, such as Kirk reports, were developed. In some cases, of course, the Church mound was originally a pagan worship site.

Page 31 . . . [the seers] . . . affirm that those Creatures that move invisibly in a house, and cast . . . great stones . . . to be Souls that have not attained their rest . . . We now come to a clear definition of supernatural activities connected to the human soul: ghostly activity (which Kirk also says is countered by the action of good spirits), is connected to the desire to reveal a wrong, or a treasure hidden, or similar unrealised desires. Kirk then tells a typical story of two women being drawn to a fairy hill and finding treasure, possibly a hoard of ancient coinage from a burial chamber. He leaves the final judgement to others, as to whether the information was conveyed by a restless soul, a good or bad angel, or a fairy messenger.

Page 32 These subterraneans have Controversies . . . As to vice and sin . . . they transgress [our laws by] . . . stealing . . . children . . . [As] for the [unfaithfulness] of the [fairy lovers] or succubi who tryst with men, it is abominable. Here Kirk is making a distinction which may be unclear to the modern reader: he basically argues that the fairies have controversies and disputes of their own, *there being some ignorance in all creatures [even] . . . the vastest created Intelligences,* but that they see no wrong in transgressing our laws when they steal away children, *which [children] never return.* Their vices, he argues, are of a higher order or more refined nature than those of men, and not bound by human laws. Thus they do not swear or drink excessively, but are prone to the emotional or spiritual vices of envy, spite and lying: the prideful sins.

The *Leannain Sith,* or fairy lemans, are mentioned by Kirk elsewhere, and he is reporting a fragment of a widespread tradition, which was that both men and women could have fairy lovers. Kirk does not mention a direct instance of a woman having a fairy lover, but he does describe a woman who was stolen away and later had a child, and this woman was examined by himself and another clergyman in person (page 37). He tells us that the fairy women take mortal lovers and abandon them cruelly, and that this is a type of refined vice among both humans and fairies. We find a similar theme in Geoffrey of Monmouth, writing in the twelfth century, where he states that *daemones* may hold intercourse with women and make them pregnant: Merlin was born of such a union, according to Geoffrey (see Appendix 7).

In its primal form this motif, especially in the context of Merlin, relates to a pagan religious mystery, the birth of a special child by a union between mortal and immortal: it is found in many myths worldwide, including of course the Christian mythos. The warning against fairy lovers is partly an orthodox religious restriction to suppress paganism, but is also found in different forms in early religious and magical texts and teachings that are non-Christian. It is perpetuated in chthonic magical arts even today, where the initiate is warned against the fatal seduction of the Otherworld men or women, but may in special circumstances, undertake such partnerships. Just as we have Co-walkers who advise or mirror the seers, we also have the more concealed tradition of the fairy marriage, with its roots in pagan ritual and myth, but operating as part of a specific Otherworldly tradition well into historical times.

The perils of having a fairy lover are amply demonstrated by the powerful magical ballad *Tam Lin* (see Appendix 3). This was preserved in collective oral tradition in Scotland at least until the nineteenth or early twentieth century, being sung by ordinary people as part of the vast repertoire of such ballads and songs that formed a grounding of mythic education and entertainment.[23]

Page 32 *As our religion obliges us not to make ... a ... curious search into these abstrusenesses* ... A list of historical or literary-mythical-historical proofs is briefly given, including a tale relating to Merlin that is not found in the medieval chronicles. Kirk is qualifying his revelation of operational traditions by drawing back a little, and reminding the reader that one must not delve too curiously into the Otherworld, but that it may be proved even by historical examples at less risk to oneself and without breaching religious rules.

Page 32 *I will next give some account of how the seer, my informer, came to have this secret way of correspondence* . . . Kirk reveals or suggests that he had at least one specific informant, a trained seer who described to him the techniques of initiation into the Second Sight. We should note that Kirk has already told us that religion forbids such curiousness, and that he is merely reporting what has been told to him by another party . . . and that, of course, he himself has nothing actively to do with seership. Yet . . .

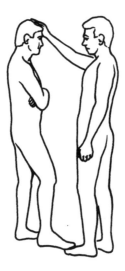

Figure 5. Initiation Position One

Page 32 *There be odd solemnities at investing a man with* . . . *the* . . . *Mystery of the Second Sight. He must run a tedder of hair* . . . *in a helix about his middle from end to end, and then bow his head downwards* . . . *and look back through his legs* . . . *or [he may] look thus back[wards] through a hole where there was a knot of fir* . . . The description is of an act of ritual magic, with many connections to magical arts in other cultures than the Gaelic. Kirk has added later notes connecting the ritual to funerary events, the hair must come from that which bound a corpse to a bier, he must look through his legs until he sees a funeral procession arriving, and crossing two marches, by which he means a boundary between two territories. These are *threshold* or *portal* ceremonies, and the childish notion of gruesome horror, such as are found in modern films and books, play no part in this type of ancient practice. As we have noted above, a major part of fairy lore is concerned with ancestors, thus the first instance of ritual is likely to be derived from pagan ceremonies of initiation involving ancestral contacts. This type of ceremony persists even today in Tibetan Buddhism, shamanism, and other chthonic religions or magical arts, and is by no means defunct.

The wearing of a helix and cord of hair (Kirk glosses *helix* as *a kind of ivy, bearing no berries, running around*) around the body has many ritual ramifications; the cord is still used in magical art today as an implement of *connection*. The helix of ivy may link to the magical powers of specific plants in folklore; ivy was an underworld plant, associated with the dead, with winter (as it remained green), and with great strength and endurance. As Kirk has added in parentheses that the hair of the tedder should be that which bound a corpse to a beir, there is an additional symbolic binding or connecting to the powers of the dead, those ancestors living in the fairy hills.

The bowing of the head to look between the legs has many connections, not the least of which are found in the Old Testament, from Jewish mystical practices. The Prophets adopted a meditative pose, just as Jewish mystics do to this day, whereby the head and feet were joined together, with the head between the legs, like a deep bow. This united the Crown, or seat of Divine Consciousness in the head, with the Kingdom, or expression of divinity in matter, the Feet. Thus the seer could foretell the future, for he united the extremes within his own body. The practice is also reminiscent of certain yoga postures, designed to enhance and realign the vital energies (see Figure 6).

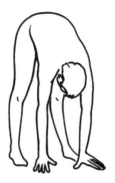

Figure 6. Initiation Position Two

Looking through the knothole of a tree is a widespread method of seeing into the other world; another method used by the women of the Stewart family was to look through the *wambe of a ring*, again involving look through a hole or defined aperture. The changing of wind puts the initiate in peril of his life, for he is in neither world at his moment of initiation and vision, so a change of circumstance in the elemental realms can leave him trapped. To this day children are told in Scotland that if the wind changes while they pull grimaces, they will be stuck so for the rest of their lives. Grimacing is frequently associated with the presence of fairies, who grimace and present ugly looks to the unwitting seers in an attempt to put them off balance or to mock them.

Page 33 *The usual method . . . to get a transient sight . . . is to put his foot on the Seer's foot, and the Seer's hand is put on the inquirer's head . . .* This position (see Figure 5) is one which Kirk disapproves of, as it implies spiritual subjection. In Kirk's day it was widely used to prove to the sceptical that there was indeed the Sight, and instances of its use are mentioned later in the text. Dr Johnson wrote that a glimpse of the Sight could be gained in exchange for tea, though one can hardly imagine him undergoing this temporary vision himself.

The implication of this transient method is that by coming within the subtle energy–field of the seer, a person without the Sight might have his or her vision stimulated for a brief moment. Kirk elaborates upon the technicalities or metaphysics (to him, science) of the Sight in several places to follow.

Page 33 *Then will he see a multitude . . . like furious hardy men flocking . . . from all Quarters, as thick as atoms in the air. These are not . . . phantasms . . . but realities appearing to a stable man . . . These [beings] . . . strike him breathless . . . but the seer . . . forbids such horror, and comforts his novice.* This is a classic description of the onset of the Second Sight, in which entities seems to boil and seethe towards the seer from all directions. The first rush passes, but is terrifying. Kirk tells us that the seer defends his pupil against horror, and even quotes a series of Biblical references concerning prophecy, Second Sight, and spiritual visions.

Having started on the Biblical defence, Kirk proceeds to develop this context on his own behalf, including an interesting interpretation of the temptation of Jesus in Matt. 4. Once again he stresses the actual visual nature of the event, and that in both seership and in the case of Jesus, it is not a phantasm or a *sick apprehension.* To round the examples off, Kirk mentions the Pythoness, priestess of the Delphic oracle of Apollo, an allusion that would have been well known to any gentleman or classical scholar from texts such as Virgil's *Aeneid.*

Page 34 *Also the seer trains his scholar by telling [him] of the gradations of nature . . . [and that the Second Sight] is a native habit in some . . . and an artificial improvement of their natural sight in others.* We have referred above to the use of natural and animal gradations or progressions on the instructions of the seers, and here Kirk expands upon the concept in detail; this system or series of entities and planes is defined again in Kirk's commentary upon Tarbett's letter (page 51 and Figure 7). He also makes the distinction between those who inherit the sight genetically, and those who acquire it artificially, through initiation, effort, or temporary admittance under the control of a skilled seer.

Page 34 *They [the seers] having such a beam [of light] continually about them, [such] as that of the sun, which when it shines . . . lets common eyes see the [dust] atoms in the air, [fragments] that*

without these rays they could not discern. This sentence refers to
the common phenomenon of dust seen when sunlight is at a
certain angle: these motes of dust were thought for a number
of centuries to be atoms, the smallest known particles. Kirk
is using this as an analogy of the beam of light about the
seers, by which he means a higher octave of light or of vision,
enabling them to see Otherworld beings just as a certain angle
or clarity of sunlight enables ordinary men to see the usually
invisible dust motes.

Page 35 *Some have this Second Sight transmitted from father to son
through the whole family, without their own consent or the teaching of
others . . . it may likewise seem strange . . . in the [cases of] seventh
sons, and others that cure . . . with only stroking of the affected part
[of the body].* Again Kirk affirms the genetic aspect of the
Second Sight, which is known to prevail in certain families
from generation to generation, as is the healing ability and
seership of seventh sons and daughters, though we find that
Kirk repeatedly limits the reporting of the ability to men, and
states (page 45) that women seldom have it. We shall return
to this comment in due course.

Page 35 *Virtue goes out from them by spirituous effluxes into the
patient . . . their vigorous healthy spirits affecting the sick, [just
as] . . . the unhealthy fumes of the sick infect the [healthy].* Kirk
suggests that a vitality or surplus of *sanative balsam* or vital
energy builds up in seventh sons, and also decreases in families
after the seventh is born. This energy is what cures the sick by
touch. We are now encountering a different concept from that
of the subterranean people, but both the Sight and healing
abilities may be conferred on certain bloodlines and on seventh
children, hence the connection. Kirk later (page 63) discusses
other means whereby certain spells, charms and practices may
be curative.

Page 35 *[Certain] minor sort of seers prognosticate . . . from the
shoulder-bone of a sheep.* This ancient practice of augury from
a mutton bone was very widespread in Celtic countries, and
may still be known today in isolated regions. It stems from the

general practice in the pagan world of using animal parts for divination,[24] and often has specific ritual lines or behaviour attached to it. Kirk observes that it is a minor art, and can only foresee for the coming month.

Page 35 *A woman, seemingly an exception from the general rule . . . and singularly wise in these matters of foresight, lived in Colonsay, an Isle of the Hebrides . . .* This story contains two levels, the first being one in which the Second Sight may mislead the seer. The woman saw correctly, but misinterpreted the direction in which invading men were rowing, and thus failed to warn her fellow islanders. This anecdote has the ring of a widespread humorous tale, based on fact, spread about to make gentle fun at the expense of the seeress.

This is one of several references by Kirk to the fact that women seldom have the Second Sight. This seems to be an unusual stance; possibly very few women would admit to it when questioned by a male priest of an authoritarian, witch-burning religion, even one as gentle and spiritually inclined as Robert Kirk. Whatever the reasons, and we note that in this tale he implies that the woman was a witch working with a familiar spirit, Kirk is not correct in this suggestion. Indeed, it is often traditionally asserted that the female bloodline passes on the Second Sight, either to daughters or sons, and not the male bloodline.

The second level concerns the nature of this woman's seership and its source. Suddenly we find a different kind of tale altogether from anything that Kirk has mentioned previously, and quite out of keeping with his general and specific thesis. Indeed, the woman from Colonsay seems to be more of a witch than a seeress, and though the two were, and are, frequently confused, Kirk himself suffered from no such confusion. . . . *as soon as she set three crosses of straw upon . . . [her] palm . . . a great ugly Beast sprang out of the Earth near her, and flew into the air . . .* She divined the answers to her requests from the Beast's limited range of behaviour, either a positive or a negative reaction. This entity sounds more like the elemental or familiar spirit well known in witchcraft and magical arts, and not a fairy entity. The ritual of the straw crosses is found in many forms worldwide where Christianity merges with a native religion or magical cult: it may have a pre-Christian origin in the very primal magical arts that use simple natural objects to conjure spirits out of the earth. Kirk suddenly leaves this seeress or witch, and proceeds to further examples more in keeping with his general thesis.

Page 36 . . . *a woman [was] taken out of her child bed, and . . . a lingering image of herself substituted . . . decayed, died, and was buried . . . but [she herself] returned to her husband after two years . . . he . . . admitted her home, and had divers children by her.* We now have a further development of the fairy nurse tradition, which Kirk seems to have had at first hand, as he says that the person lived in the region next to his own parish. In several of the major aspects of his thesis, Kirk returns to further examples or developments of his early examples as he progresses: in this case the stolen woman was blinded in one eye by the fairies for using a magical ointment which enabled her to see them.

Page 37 *[But before they blinded her] she found the place full of light without any . . . lamp.* Kirk returns again to the theme of the perpetual lamps or magical light found in the underworld or in fairy dwellings. The substitution of a false body for the missing human, which dies and is buried accordingly, is often thought to be a rationalisation of wasting illnesses, such as tuberculosis which was endemic in the Highlands of Scotland. Yet we have this peculiar tale of a wife that returned after her wasting-double has been buried: Kirk offers no further explanation for it, and does not go into the nature of the wasting image that is substituted for the human woman or child in such abductions. The main value for him in this tale seems to be the account of the fairy realm.

Robert Kirk now writes one of the most cryptic and tantalising lines in his entire book:

Page 37 *There is an art apparently without superstition for recovering of [people] such as are thus stolen, but I think it superfluous to insert it [here].* Kirk himself died on 14 May 1692: local tradition asserts that he collapsed while walking at night on the fairy hill at

Aberfoyle. Some time after his death and burial, however, Kirk appeared to a relative and gave a detailed set of instructions by the means of which he might be recovered from the fairy realm. He was not, therefore, dead at all, and could be retrieved at the christening ceremony of his own (posthumous) infant. The ritual for his recovery was that he would appear at the christening, and his cousin was to throw a knife over him which would liberate him (due presumably to the fairies' aversion to iron). In 1812 Patrick Graham[25] wrote that local people firmly believed that Kirk was still in fairyland, as his cousin had been so astonished at his appearance at the christening, that he had failed to throw the knife as advised. The tradition persisted into the twentieth century, and was noted by W.Y. Evans Wentz.[1]

The usual position of folklorists on this subject is that it is an attachment of fairy traditions to the local priest who had shown such great interest in them during his lifetime.

Kirk himself believed in both the physical and spiritual translation of a person into the fairy realm, and clearly defined the differences between these two modes: there are also many hints throughout his text of an ancient initiatory magical tradition concerning the relationships between humans and fairies, and the presence of ancestral spirits in fairy hills. Kirk, as we have noted, was a seventh son, and may have had, or certainly was believed by his parishioners to have had, healing powers.

The attachment of physical or spiritual translation at his death, therefore, is not an idle superstition, but an expression of a deep-rooted tradition which stems back to pagan and prehistoric cultures. The connection to his reappearance at the posthumous christening of his child has resonances of the ballad of *Tam Lin*, for the birth of a child and the death or rebirth of a man are, as Kirk himself reported, part of the revolution of the Wheel of Life. Tam Lin (see page 26) is also connected to the ancient theme of magical guardianship of a sacred site, in which the spirit of a mortal is set to guard a powerful location until summoned back to the human world.

In Kirk's case his spirit still guards the fairy hill at Aberfoyle: Tam Lin (not known to be a historical person) guarded a sacred wood and well; Thomas Rhymer (certainly a historical person) was connected to the fairy hills of Eildon, by Melrose in the Scottish Borders, under which the gates into Elfland were to be found; Merlin (possibly several historical prophets bearing a generic title) may still be met at Dinas Emrys in North Wales, but not in Glastonbury where modern pseudo-traditions have wrongly placed him. The location of guardians upon a site is not simply that of great emperors or kings, such as Bladud (legendary god-king at Aquae Sulis), Arthur of the Britains, or Barbarossa,[27] but also of humble priests such as Robert Kirk, and many others unknown by name, but perhaps encountered by those of the Second Sight to this day.

Page 37 *I saw a woman of forty years [of] age . . . she took . . . little or no food . . . she tarried in the fields overnight . . . conversed with a people [that] she knew not . . . slept upon a hillock, found herself transported to another place before day. [She] had a child since that time . . .* Once again we have the tale of transportation, invisible people, and possibly a case in which the woman believed herself to have conceived as a result of the fairy adventure. Kirk, who takes pains to clarify that he examined her in the company of another clergyman and not alone, says that her energies were balanced, like an inextinguishable lamp or like those of hibernating creatures in winter.

Page 37 *It is usual in all magical arts to have the candidates prepossessed with a belief of their tutor's skill . . . But a person called Stewart, possessed with a prejudice against . . . this Second Sight . . . was so put to it by a seer before many witnesses, that he lost his speech . . . because of the many fearful wights appearing unto him . . .* The example here, which Kirk says occurred near to his own house, shows a sceptic being put to the test, or as the sceptic thought, putting the Second Sight to the test. Kirk has already given us the methods by which this is achieved (page 33), and if we grant this to be one event of which the author had first-hand knowledge it clearly proves his theory that one does not have to believe in the Second Sight or the fairy people to experience them. This is followed by two further examples, one involving a sceptical clergyman and Highland seer, and the other a very trivial event, possibly a practical joke.

LORD TARBETT'S LETTER TO THE HONOURABLE ROBERT BOYLE

A succinct account of my Lord of Tarbett's relations in a letter to the Honourable Robert Boyle Esquire, of the predictions made by a seer whereof himself was ear and eye witness. Kirk gives an entire account of Tarbett's letter, then argues against several of the points made in it. As has been suggested in the Introduction (page 3) this letter may have part of the curiosity shown towards seership in terms of military intelligence: perhaps the most important general aspect of it is that Tarbett began by disbelieving in the Sight, but was convinced by so many examples both in his own experience and as reported to him. Robert Boyle, one of the founders of modern chemistry developing out of alchemy, was interested in apparitions at that time, and is known to have written a paper on encounters experienced by miners while working underground.

Page 39 *Many Highlanders, [and] yet . . . more Islanders were qualified with this Second Sight . . . men women and children indistinctly [that is indiscriminately] were subject to it . . . It is a trouble to most . . . and they would be rid of it . . . if they could.* Here Tarbett differs from Kirk, stating (correctly) that men, women and children may experience the Sight indiscriminately.

Page 39 *The Sight is of no long duration . . . The hardy . . . fix their look that they may see longer . . .* Tarbett observes that certain individuals trained their faculty to be able to see for longer periods without their eyes watering or *twinkling*, while the timorous have eyes that water immediately they experience the Sight. The watering of eyes or involuntary tears are a hallmark of prophetic consciousness. Tears of prophecy are found in many religious traditions, and were associated with the influential Prophecies of Merlin, who, according to

Geoffrey of Monmouth, burst into tears as he uttered the future history of Britain.

Page 39 *some of the hardiest and the longest [in] experience have some rules for conjectures [of interpretation of their visions].* Tarbett makes a further distinction between the dedicated or hardy seers, who focus the vision, and establish rules of interpretation, and those to whom the Sight is a brief, frightening, involuntary experience. He then gives a number of contemporary examples, both from his own experience and from that reported by others of good character. It is interesting to note that many of his examples involve displacement of an event in time, very simple matters of seeing something a year or a few days or even an hour before it occurs. These visions are of a slightly different emphasis than the fairy traditions reported by Kirk, who seems more concerned with the subterranean dimension, the esoteric philosophy, and the possibilities of physical transportation and translation or conception between fairy and human. Tarbett's account is, as stated in the title, succinct, dwelling upon practical matters.

He then conjectures the reasons for the Sight, and provides us with a valuable piece of information, which Kirks takes up, disputes, and amplifies in his response.

Page 44 *. . . several . . . [with] the Second Sight . . . when transported to . . . other countries, especially . . . America . . . quite lost this quality* . . . The implication here is that the Sight is connected to the land, is somehow environmental. Kirk disputes Tarbett's interpretation of this loss, but confirms it to be connected to the land (see page 114 below).

KIRK'S COMMENTARY UPON TARBETT'S LETTER

Page 45 *But a few women are endowed with this Sight.* Kirk immediately disputes Tarbett's findings concerning the diffusion of the Sight, possibly due to the connection between women seers and the fanatical obsessions with witchcraft that had been prevalent in Scotland and England for many years.

Only a few years before Kirk assembled his treatise, Major Weir and his sister had been executed in Edinburgh in 1670 for magical, necromantic, incestuous, and Otherworldly practices. In her case, she freely admitted consorting with the Queen of Elfland who taught her supernatural skills in weaving. This famous trial and execution was all the more remarkable because Weir had long been an earnest Covenanter (one of the active political Protestant movements of the time), and commander of the Edinburgh city guard during the ascendancy of the puritanical revolutionary Commonwealth government. These conflicts, incidentally, are the wars involving the English that Tarbett refers to in his letter (page 41). Sir Walter Scott recorded the sister's last words at execution as being, 'Many weep and lament for a poor old wretch like me, but alas few are weeping for a broken covenant.' If Scott's nineteenth-century report draws upon true sources, then it seem likely that she was talking not of her brother's erstwhile Christianity, but of her own pact with the Otherworld, and the general antagonism towards such covenants.

Kirk then repeats his basic thesis, that the Sight is not criminal, that ancestral spirits appear to seers, that the fairy people create visions for the seers, rather than the visions being *similitudes* of the actual objects or persons seen. This is not mentioned by Tarbett at all, and indeed he is not concerned with the traditions of the fairies, only with the Sight itself.

Page 46 . . . *this Sight can be no quality of the air [as suggested by Tarbett], nor the eyes, because . . . such as live in the same air . . . have not the second sight.* Kirk argues against Tarbett's suggestion that the clean air of the Highlands and Islands induces Second Sight, and cites the obvious fact that people in the same region may not have it, yet a seer can temporarily induce it. All of this is affirmed in his thesis of the subterranean people.

Page 47 . . . *some . . . pierce and kill [with their eye] whatever creature they first [see]* . . . This is the first example of the evil eye (which was also investigated in Spain by Samuel Pepys in 1684) mentioned by Kirk. He introduces it as a disproof of

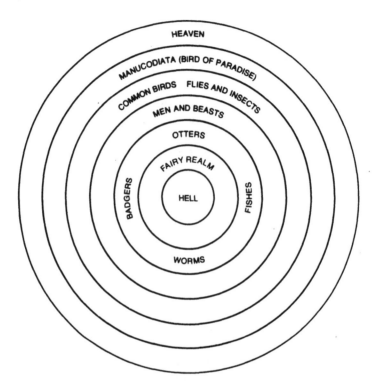

HEAVEN

MANUCODIATA (BIRD OF PARADISE)

COMMON BIRDS   FLIES AND INSECTS

MEN AND BEASTS

OTTERS

FAIRY REALM

BADGERS

HELL

FISHES

WORMS

Figure 7. Robert Kirk's Cosmology and Hierarchy of
Birds, Animals, Humans and Fairies

Tarbett's' suggestions as to cause of the Sight. A man with this
ability to blast by looking, says Kirk, speaking from experience
of a case, may not be a seer, or see anything more than usual
with his regular eyesight. Kirk suggests, therefore, that the evil
eye is not connected to the Second Sight, and is not part of the
communion between fairy and human beings. He does not make
any suggestions as to its origins, other than the fact that the
person so cursed may be *radicated in malice*. This would presume
a type of telepathy or involuntary transfer of negative energy.

Page 47 . . . *the true solution . . . seems . . . to be as follows* . . . Kirk
summarises his own ideal statement on the Second Sight, in
what was for him, perhaps, a very important declaration,

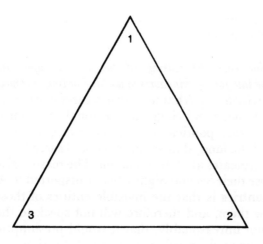

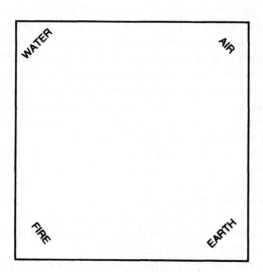

Figure 8. The Power of Seven: Showing the
Supernal or Divine Trinity

that the communion between the worlds was a proof against atheism and materialism.

Page 48 *Nor does the ceasing of the visions, upon the seer's transmigration into foreign kingdoms make his Lordship's conjecture . . . a whit more probable . . .* What follows is a careful presentation of the theory of guardian beings on a regional or national scale, not in any childish political or symbolic sense, but in terms of the holism of the land, that same concept of sacred and divine Land that permeates ancestral religion. The reason, Kirk says, that seers lose their Second Sight when transported to America or other countries is that the invisible entities of those lands do not know them, and therefore will not speak to them. He then says, not unreasonably, that it would presumptuous for the Scots alone to claim sole possession of the Sight.

Kirk is, of course, correct in all of this argument, though the modern reader might not appreciate his Biblical presentation of certain proofs. Otherworld traditions are, as he says, found in every country, and are always connected to entities that are attuned to the land itself, often seeming to reach into the distant prehistoric or dreaming past. A seer with a Co-walker will lose that companion when abroad, but may in time, as Kirk suggests, come to some acquaintance with the spirits of the lands in which he or she find themselves.

Now follows a series of Biblical citations concerning the subtle or aery body. The concept of Elemental Air should not be confused with gaseous air, but is used repeatedly by Kirk to define the lightest and most mobile of materialised energies. Thus Air and bodies of Air are really the highest octave of matter, so light, subtle and changeable that it may not be seen without special visual faculties.

Following the Biblical citations, we find the classical sources of authority for Kirk's thesis: *Pythagoras, Socrates, Plato, Dionysus Areopagita,* and *the Poets.* And if we doubt Kirk's learning at all after this array of evidence, he cites Dr Moore, and Cornelius Agrippa. Agrippa (1486–1535) is perhaps the most curious reference in the list, for he was notorious as a magician. Possibly Kirk is referring to Agrippa's *De Occulta Philosophia,* published in 1531.

Various examples concerning the protection of humans by invisible allies are given (page 50) such as the *noctambulo* or sleep-walker who suffers no injury. The strumpet *Leannain Sith*, or fairly lemans, are reintroduced, and the curious phenomenon of Highlanders stabbing their companions as a result of temporary possession by *our aerial neighbours*.

Page 50 *I [will] add but one instance more of a very young maid, who . . . learned a large piece of poetry by the frequent repetition of it, from one of our nimble and courteous spirits . . . I have a copy of it.* There are several traditions involving the learning of poetry, spells, and musical skill from the fairies. In Kirk's example he says that the maiden learned, by heart, a set of verse partly pious and partly superstitious, so we may presume that it was one of the Gaelic prayers or spells that abounded in the Highlands.[28] *Yet no person was ever heard to repeat it before, nor was the maid capable to compose it of her self.*

We may consider several possibilities to this tradition of learning from Otherworldly beings – a tradition that is still active today in many parts of the world. A typical modern example is well known in the Southern United States, concerning the learning of guitar skills from the Devil, who may be encountered at a crossroads, according to certain blues musicians. Ancient poets certainly expected that spirits would contact them in sacred places and inspire poetry; in Scotland the Macrimmond pipers are widely said to have learned skills from the fairies, as had certain fiddlers. We have already mentioned Thomas Rhymer who learned prophetic arts and poetic skills in Elfland.

It is possible that this poetic or inspirational tradition was mixed with a certain amount of formal instruction, by which prayers and spells were secretly taught to novices under mysterious circumstances. Techniques are taught traditionally for making contact with Otherworldly beings, often at ancient sites: such techniques result in the learning of skills, verses, or in subtle gifts such as magical powers.

Kirk now repeats his main theory concerning the underworld realms, and the possibility of bodies or vehicles lighter and less visible than our own. He returns to the concept of universal and terrestrial holism, with a subterranean counter-part.

Page 51 *The Manucodiata or Bird of Paradise, living in the highest region of the air; Common Birds in the Second Region . . . [and so downwards through various orders of being] can we then think the middle cavities of the Earth to be empty?* Kirk's cosmology is (see Figure 7) similar to that of Renaissance adepts, drawing upon various traditional and Neoplatonic sources. Similar sets of harmonic or hierarchical relationships are found in many publications from the sixteenth to the nineteenth century, and earlier variants are found in medieval texts, often in complex written form with no illustration, though illustrations also occur. Earlier cosmic figures or maps are known, of course, from Roman, Greek, Egyptian, Babylonian and Assyrian cultures, so the concept of interlinked or concentric levels of entities or worlds is inherent in human consciousness.

Kirk's model is very close to the cosmology described in detail in the twelfth-century *Vita Merlini*, which, like Kirk's own book, was based upon Celtic oral tradition. While the *Vita* was based upon bardic poems and tales concerning Merlin, as amended and expanded by Geoffrey of Monmouth, Kirk's lore is based mainly on direct reports from ordinary people. Yet the world-view and magical cosmology, with its holistic concepts and assertion of communion between human and underworld beings, is shared by both.

Ancient burial mounds and caverns in Scotland, Eng-land, and Malta are then cited as physical evidence of the underworld people. Though we discount this today as physical evidence, such sites are still regarded as centres of energy, ancestral contact, and for attuning to the forces of nature. Indeed, there is a considerable revival of interest in the subtle levels of sacred sites today, such as Kirk himself virtually predicted when he said that humanity's relationship with and perception of the subterranean people would eventually be as widespread as any modern device once frowned upon as magical but soon proven to be perfectly normal. This argument is used several times by Kirk, and has certain merits in simultaneously dissolving prejudice and superstition.

Page 52 *I have found five curiosities in Scotland, not much observed to be [known] elsewhere* . . . The five curiosities are as follows:

1. The labour of the Brownies (previously discussed).

2. The Mason Word. Here Kirk is referring to the tradition that certain so-called ancient aspects of Masonry are known in Scotland, and that Scottish Masonry is of a more original lineage than that of England, having unique elements to it, such as the Mason Word.

3. The Second Sight.

4. Curative charms (see page 63)

5. Magical proof against wounding used by Scottish soldiers.

With the possible exception of the Scottish Mason Word, these curiosities are found worldwide in various folk traditions, albeit taking varied forms.

Page 54 *Though I will not be so curious nor so peremptory as he who will [seek to] prove . . . the Philosopher's Stone from Scripture . . . or the plurality of Worlds . . . or the circulation of the blood . . . nor the Talismanical Art . . . Yet I humbly propose these passages which may give some light to our subject* . . . First Kirk disclaims a list of passages as possible proofs of obscure subjects revealed by the Bible, thus encouraging us to look such passages up immediately. His choice is in some cases rather a curious one, and well worth pursuing. He then proposes a further list of passages which he considers allowable to prove subjects such as *Daemones Loci; spirits; seeing at a distance; and the power of the name of Jesus over subterranean inhabitants* which is also discussed in this Commentary on page 89.

The list of quotations is worth reading in full, as it gives us an insight into Kirk's extremely fluid and subtle use of the Bible. His argument had to be based upon grounds that contemporary authorities would accept, therefore he includes science and firm analysis and discussion, with irrefutable Biblical evidence. We need to remember that the Bible was taken literally by most people of the seventeenth century, and that to suggest that most of it was a carefully edited reworking of mythology and Semitic folklore would have been shocking, sacrilegious and, of course, punishable. Furthermore, no such sacrilegious thought was ever in Kirk's mind: he was a deeply Christian priest, seeking the fusion of undeniable seership and healing powers with the Christian spiritual revelation and code of ethics.

Kirk suggests the ancient division of Good, Evil, and Intermediate Spirits, which was known to both pagan and Christian philosophers. It leads us to the following concept:

Page 54 . . . *[the good spirits] relinquishing us . . . upon our neglect [of virtue] . . . [but] None of [these bad spirits] having power to compel us to any misdemeanour without our flat consent.* Kirk tells us that a seer attuned to good thoughts and deeds will attract beneficial companions from the underworld, but that negative, lustful thoughts and images will attract a malicious spirit or a bad angel. He returns to this theme later. After further Biblical arguments, Kirk feels ready to tackle *the most obvious objections against the . . . lawfulness of this speculation.* Is the Second Sight witchcraft? No, because it comes often as a natural faculty and not through spells or compacts with evil spirits.

Pages 55–6 . . . *it is not a sense wholly adduced to Scripture to say that this Second Sight . . . has some vestige in Holy Writ; but rather [that] it is modestly adduced from it.* Finally Kirk makes a gentle retreat, but not too far, for having loaded the reader with Biblical proof, he withdraws slightly, to allow us not to become prejudiced against his argument by the sheer weight of his evidence. Nor is this simply a modest demurral, for throughout the text there is always caution against charges of heresy, magic, immorality, and so forth. The discussion concerning procreation and nourishment of the fairy people is developed further, and the questions then move to a subtle subject:

Page 56 *In the process of time we may come to converse as familiarly with [the fairy people] . . . as we do now with the Chinese and Antipodes.* Kirk proposes a future in which any suggestion of unnaturalness or witchcraft is dispelled by the simple fact that communion between the superterranean and subterranean people will be commonplace.

The subject of vices, lusts and passions among the fairy people is reassessed, and Kirk reminds us that the spread of the Gospel has dispelled many of the more barbarous superstitious practices of paganism, yet the Sight itself remains. He then returns to the matter of purity in seership:

Page 57 *A concurrence they [the fairy people] have to what is virtuously done, for upon committing of a foul deed, one will find a demur upon his Soul, as if his cheerful Colleague had deserted him.* Although this statement may seem superficially similar to concepts of good and evil qualities in orthodox religion, it is a precise and technical magical statement. Here is the key to the connection between the seer and his allies or Co-walkers, for the consciousness or spiritual quality of the seer attunes the contact. If we commit a foul deed, the Co-walker may desert us. In magical arts there are many strict prohibitions relating to spirit contacts, and much of the basic training consists in attuning the imagination and general behaviour to resonate within a specific Mystery or conceptual model. When this is successfully undertaken, the Otherworldly contacts come alive. When it is broken or lapsed, they vanish.

As an artistic magical or spiritual discipline, such a model consists of a fusion of the forces of the imagination with carefully defined patterns of living, ethical behaviour, diet, habits, location in sacred places, and so forth. Kirk is, of course, highly ethical, and is only interested in promoting contact with well-intentioned entities, but the techniques may be used for both good or ill, as he himself tells us.

Page 58 *Does the acquiring of this Second Sight make any change on the acquirer's body mind or actions? Answer: All uncouth sights enfeeble the Seer.* Biblical evidence is again cited, but Kirk proceeds to say that initially the seer is put into a transport similar to death. After this initiatory experience, only foolish, illiterate people are frightened by the visions. Once again we have implications here of a specific training: certain seers, after the death-like transport of their first experience, can train their will to work with the Second Sight and the fairy contacts: but *clownish* men cannot handle the experience.

Page 59 *Does not Satan interpose . . . by many subtle unthought-of insinuations . . .? Answer: The goodness of the life and designs of the ancient Prophets and Seers was one of the best proofs of their mission* . . . Kirk then adds the significant point (supported by the observations of Tarbett and others who studied the Sight at first hand), that the seers do not necessarily perform anything, but act as neutral observers through their heightened faculties.

Kirk now returns to the historical argument that many new inventions or discoveries are not sinful in themselves, only if they are used for evil. He repeatedly asserts the neutrality of the Sight, and argues against theoretical questions concerning its sinfulness. Next he tackles the problem of Original Sin and returns again to the genetic aspects of the faculty of Second Sight and healing abilities. He points out that the children of seers do not inherit any evil tendencies, as they might if theirs was a diabolical compact . . . and that many other people suddenly acquire the sight, as Tarbett also observes.

CONCLUSION

Kirk's set of conclusions in the text is actually a summary of the basic traditional elements of the Second Sight and fairy lore, without any of the more subtle aspects embedded within the main thesis.

By way of conclusion to this brief commentary, we might consider Kirk's seemingly cautious or ambivalent attitude to women as seers, and to the *Leannain Sith* or fairy lovers, who, he says in his Conclusion, conjoin with mortals to produce Merlin-like offspring. I would suggest from the implications of the text, though there is no hard proof, that Robert Kirk was well aware that seership was commonplace among women, and that one of the 'secrets' of Second Sight and magical arts was the sexual union of humans and Otherworld entities such as fairies. This sexual or polarity magic, even between humans, is still regarded as a dark and mysterious subject today, when many people claim to be re-establishing a revival of paganism, though it was originally one of the basic practices of pagan religion.

We need, somehow, to dispel repressive Christian conditioning in this context, clearly something which Kirk could not state in any way in his thesis, assuming that he thought in such terms in the first place, which is unlikely. Such liberation from repression does not consist of sexual or magical irresponsibility, but of simplicity and clarity of direction, just as Kirk himself reminds us when stating that a demur upon the soul will cause the Companion to depart.

APPENDIX 1

Extract from an Essay on the origins of the Rosicruscians and Freemasons, by Thomas De Quincey in his collected writings, *Suspiria De Profundis*, 1871.

There are a number of significant connections between Fairy lore in European tradition, Robert Kirk's *Secret Commonwealth* and the imagery employed by the original seventeenth century Rosicrucian texts.

The second work gives an account of such a society as already established: this is the celebrated work entitled *Fama Fraternitatis of the meritorious order of the Rosy Cross, addressed to the learned in general and the Governors of Europe*; and here we are presented with the following narrative: – Christian Rosycross, of noble descent, having upon his travels into the East and into Africa learned great mysteries from Arabians, Chaldeans, etc., upon his return to Germany established, in some place not mentioned, a secret society composed at first of four – afterwards of eight – members, who dwelt together in a building (called the House of the Holy Ghost) erected by him: to these persons, under a vow of fidelity and secrecy, he communicated his mysteries. After they had been instructed, the society dispersed agreeably to their destination, with the exception of two members, who remained alternately with the founder. The rules of the order were these: 'The members were to cure the sick without fee or reward. No member to wear a peculiar habit, but to dress after the fashion of the country. On a certain day in every year all the members to assemble in the House of the Holy Ghost, or to account for their absence. Every member to appoint some person with the proper qualifications to succeed him at his own decease.

The word *Rosy-Cross* to be their seal, watch-word, and characteristic mark. The association to be kept unrevealed for a hundred years.' Christian Rosycross died at the age of 106 years. His death was known to the society, but not his grave: for it was a maxim of the first Rosicrucians to conceal their burial-places even from each other. New masters were continually elected into the House of the Holy Ghost; and the society had now lasted 120 years. At the end of this period a door was discovered in the house, and upon the opening of this door a sepulchral-vault. Upon the door was this inscription: One hundred and twenty years hence I shall open (*Post CXX annos patebo.*) The vault was a heptagon. Every side was five feet broad and eight feet high. It was illuminated by an artificial sun. In the centre was placed instead of a grave-stone a circular altar with a little plate of brass, whereon these words were inscribed: This grave, an abstract of the whole world, I made for myself whilst yet living (A.C.R.C. Hoc Universi compendium vivus mihi sepulchrum feci). About the margin was – To me Jesus is all in all (Jesus mihi omnia). In the centre were four figures enclosed in a circle by this revolving legend: Nequaquam vacuum legis jugum. Libertas Evangelii. Dei gloria intacta. (The empty yoke of the law is made void. The liberty of the gospel. The unsullied glory of God.) Each of the seven sides of the vault had a door opening into a chest; which chest, besides the secret books of the order and the *Vocabularium* of Paracelsus, contained also mirrors – little bells – burning lamps – marvellous mechanisms of music, etc., all so contrived that after the lapse of many centuries, if the whole order should have perished, it might be re-established by means of this vault. Under the altar, upon raising the brazen tablet, the brothers found the body of Rosycross, without taint or corruption. The right hand held a book written upon vellum with golden letters: this book, which is called T., has since become the most precious jewel of the society next after the Bible; and at the end stand subscribed the names of the eight brethren, arranged in two separate circles, who were present at the death and burial of Father Rosycross. Immediately after the above narrative follows a declaration of their mysteries addressed by the society to the whole world. They profess themselves to be of the Protestant faith; that they honour the Emperor and the laws of the Empire; and that the art of gold-making is but a slight object with them, and a mere πάρεργον. The whole work ends with these words: – 'Our House of the Holy Ghost, though a hundred thousand men should have looked upon it, is yet destined to remain untouched, imperturbable, out of sight, and unrevealed to the whole godless world for ever.'

APPENDIX 2

The Lyke Wake Dirge: a traditional dirge from the North of England

This song was traditionally sung over a corpse, and represents a psychopompic or post-mortem tradition similar to that reported by Kirk as current in seventeenth-century Scotland.

THE LYKE WAKE DIRGE
Or Chant sung by those keeping watch over a corpse

Refrain lines are sung in every verse.

> This ae nighte, this ae nighte,
> *Every nighte and alle,*
> Fire and sleet and candle-lighte,
> *And Christe receive thy saule.*

> When from here thou art past,
> *Every nighte and alle,*
> To Whinny-muir thou comest at last,
> *And Christe receive thy saule*

> If ever thou gavest hosen and shoon
> Sit thee doun and put them on

> If hosen and shoon thiu gavest nane,
> The whinnes shall pricke thee to the bare bane

> From Whinny-muir when thou art past
> To Brigg o' Dread thou comest at last

From Brigg o' Dread when thou art past
To Purgatory fire thou comest at last

If ever thou gavest meat or drinke
The fires shall never make thee shrink

If meat or drink thou gavest nane
The fire shall burn thee to the bare bane

(From *Songs of The North*, ed. Macleod and Boulton 8th ed.,
The Leadenhall Press London n.d.)

APPENDIX 3

Tam Lin, a narrative magical ballad from Scottish tradition.

This ballad, from oral collective tradition, has a number of European parallels, and contains many aspects of fairy or Otherworld lore as described by Robert Kirk.

YOUNG TAM LIN
Traditional Scottish ballad

The King forbade his maidens a'
That wore gold in their hair
To come and go by Carterhaugh,
For the young Tam Lin is there.

And those that go by Carterhaugh
From them he takes a fee,
Either their rings or their mantles
Or else their maidenheads!

So Janet has kilted her green mantle
Just a little above her knee,
And she has gone to Carterhaugh
Just as fast as she could flee.

She had not pulled a double rose,
A rose but three or four,
When up and spoke this young Tam Lin,
Crying 'Lady, pull no more!'

'How dare you pull those flowers!
How dare you break those wands!
How dare you come to Carterhaugh
Withouten my command?'

She says, 'Carterhaugh it is my own
My Father gave it me,
And I will come and go by here
Withouten any leave of thee!'

There were four and twenty ladies gay
All sitting down at chess,
In and come the fair young Janet,
As pale as any glass.

Up and spake her father dear,
He spake up meek and mild,
'Oh alas, Janet,' he cried,
'I fear you go with child!'

'And if I go with child,
It is myself to blame!
There's not a lord in all your hall
Shall give my child his name!'

Janet has kilted her green mantle
Just a little above her knee,
And she has gone to Carterhaugh
For to pull the scathing tree.

'How dare you pull that herb
All among the leaves so green
For to kill the bonny babe
That we got us between!'

'You must tell to me Tam Lin,
Ah you must tell to me,
Were you once a mortal knight
Or mortal hall did see?'

'I was once a mortal knight
I was hunting here one day,
I did fall from off my horse,
The Fairy Queen Stole me away.

'And pleasant is the Fairy land
But a strange tale I'll tell,
For at the end of seven years
They pay a fine to Hell.

'At the end of seven years
They pay a fine to Hell,
And as I am of mortal flesh
I fear it is myself.'

'Tomorrow night is Halloween,
And the Fairy Folk do ride;
Those that would their true love win
At Miles Cross they must hide!

'First you let pass the black horse
Then you let pass the brown,
But run up to the milk white steed
And pull the rider down.

'First they'll change me in your arms
Into some snake or adder,
Hold me close and fear me not,
For I'm your child's father.

'Then they'll turn me in your arms
Into a lion wild,
Hold me close and fear me not
As you would hold your child.

'Then they'll turn me in your arms
Into a red-hot bar of iron,
Hold me close and fear me not
For I will do no harm.

'Then they'll turn me in your arms
Into some burning lead,
Throw me into well-water
And throw me in with speed.

'Last they'll turn me in your arms
Into a naked knight
Wrap me up in your green mantle,
And hide me close from sight.'

So well she did what he did say
She did her true love win,
She wrapped him up in her mantle,
As blythe as any bird in Spring.

Up and spake the Fairy Queen,
And angry cried she,
'If I'd have known of this Tam Lin,
That some lady'd borrowed thee,

'If I had known of this Tam Lin,
That some lady borrowed thee,
I'd have plucked out thine eyes of flesh
And put in eyes from a tree!

'If I'd have known of this Tam Lin,
Before we came from home,
I'd have plucked out thine heart of flesh
And put in a heart of stone!'

YOUNG TAM LIN

This ballad, found only in Scottish tradition is of major importance to a full realisation of the under world tradition. The following elements are particularly significant.

1. Maidens with gold in their hair
The heroine is a virgin within a collection of virgins.

2. Green mantle
Wearing of green is associated with magic, witchcraft and fertility. 'A green gown' is the traditional term for rustic defloration, and overall the wearing of green is associated with earth-magic. Thomas the Rhymer is given clothing of green by the Queen of Elfland. The significance within the tradition is that the wearing of green signifies unity with the Land. Janet's virgin state, therefore, is no mere human condition, but declares her to be a character such as the epiphanies of the Goddess or Spirit of the Land that occur in

early Celtic poetical convention. It is her true love that later wins Tam Lin back to humanity.

3. Pulling of Flowers

Tam Lin is summoned by pulling of roses and the breaking of branches. He is therefore an Otherworld guardian who may be summoned or aroused through magic connected to Nature. He states that none should come to Carterhaugh without his own command, and we note from verse 2 that he takes a fee from trespassers. His role is that of the ex-human attuned to an environmental site by magical power. At this stage, he appears as a threatening being to unwitting visitors to his hill (Carterhaugh). Janet, however, lays claim to the site, *through the gift of her father the King.*

4. Carterhaugh

As with other examples from Scottish tradition, Carterhaugh is an actual location, in Selkirkshire. The insistence upon actual locations in the outer-world is central to the tradition. In Walter Scott's day, local people insisted that 'fairy rings' upon Carterhaugh, which stands at the conflux of the rivers Yarrow and Ettrick, were evidence of the magical struggle for liberty. Similar traditions are linked to the Reverend Robert Kirk of Aberfoyle, and to Thomas of Ercledoune, both historical characters with documented backgrounds. In other parts of Britain, folk tradition has often been proven by archaeological excavation, particularly where local customs and tales provide rationalisations that preserve memory of pre-Christian worship and burial sites.

5. Tam Lin is both physical and non-physical

In various versions of the ballad, verses occur (not included in the text above) which present the dual nature of Tam Lin – his presence in both worlds.

> When she came to Carterhaugh
> Tam Lin was at the well
> And there she found his steed standing
> But away was himsel.

This duality occurs again in verses where Tam Lin and Janet make love, during which she 'falls in a mist' and her lover is both present and 'away'. In several variants of the story, Tam Lin is enchanted at or by a magical well. His horse may be found by the well, as a sign or totem symbol of his presence, but he is present *in another dimension*, that of Elfland, fairyland, the Otherworld or under world. He is summoned by the pulling of roses, and it should be noted in this context that

plants and trees are the routes whereby spirits are enabled to return
to the womb for rebirth, in primal tradition.

6. Janet becomes pregnant

Despite Tam Lin's seeming insubstantiality, Janet 'goes with child',
and will not acknowledge any mortal origin for her condition. This
pregnancy is significant in several ways, over and above the obvious
allusion to pagan fertility magic. There is a strong parallel between
Janet's pregnancy 'in a mist' and the actual translation of Tam Lin
from fairyland. The ballads imply that the two processes are possibly
united or analogous. Folk tradition does not necessarily discriminate
between magical location of beings, the spirits of the dead, and the
birth of children. From an esoteric viewpoint, within the more subtle
teachings of the tradition, the popular lore is not, in fact, 'confused'.
Nor are we suggesting that the ballad lore is merely a folk restatement
of the so-called 'laws of reincarnation', for the true implication of
the tradition is one of synchronicity and correspondence through
more than one world, with primary motivations devolving from a
key archetype that may be expressed in more than one mode.

7. Four-and-twenty ladies gay

The chess-playing ladies or maidens appear in several variants in
Tam Lin. They are often placed in fairyland, as an example of the
joys of that place. In our particular version of the ballad, they are at
the court of the King, but in either case they represent the collection
of feminine powers at work. Chess, it should be remembered, was no
mere diversion, but a magical or cosmological game in Celtic culture.
The regular appearance of chess-playing maidens in ancient lore,
both folk and literary, may suggest that they are 'fates' or operative
powers of creation and destruction.

8. Janet seeks for Tam Lin

In the variant given above, Janet seeks to abort her child by pulling
a specific herb. The presence of plants of fertility and of abortive
power is common in traditional material, for all the obvious reasons;
but there is a magical element or correspondence at work in this
juxtaposition of herbs which should not be ignored.

What is particularly significant in this context is Janet's motivation
for her actions. She has refused to acknowledge any mortal knight
as father of her child, even hinting at a supernatural or immaculate
conception ('And if I go with child,/ It is myself to blame! . . .'), yet
she seeks to abort, and so summons Tam Lin. As soon as he appears,
she asks him his *origins*, either his mortality, or in some variants, his
Christianity.

It is worth reconsidering the action that precedes this event.

    (a)   Janet wilfully seeks the enchanted hill or well, having been warned that Tam Lin will take a fee, or her maidenhead.

    (b)   She summons him intentionally by pulling roses.

    (c)   They become lovers; in some versions in a magical mist.

    (d)   Janet returns home, and discovers that she is pregnant.

    (e)   She refuses to be married off to a mortal, and returns to Carterhaugh, 'to pull the scathing tree'.

    (f)   Tam Lin appears to stop her aborting the child.

    (g)   *She asks him his identity*, his true origin.

Janet's question is the key to the whole magical process. Prior to the question, Tam Lin is a guardian of the sacred hill, well or roses. He will impregnate maidens, after the manner of the ancient 'fertility Mysteries', and then disappear. Note that the result of 'pulling forbidden roses' is pregnancy; but this is not a moralistic or Christian warning by any means. Pregnancy results from pulling roses without permission from the guardian – in other words, perpetuating the blind powers of procreation without understanding.

    To gain permission from the guardian, one has to know his name, which in magical operations involves *asking the correct questions*. Indeed, the 'name' is the sum of all the answers to the correct questions, and is a quality or mode of awareness rather than a mere label.

    Janet seeks, therefore, to *stop* the regular cycle of creation, by her act of abortion. This willed turning away from the regular flow of events summons Tam Lin. Unlike his last manifestation, he is immediately trapped by her magical question, which is '*What is your origin?*' From this turning point, the entire tone and direction of the ballad changes. The Otherworld guardian reveals his true nature: that of an enchanted man entrapped within a magical realm and cycle from which he cannot escape by his own efforts.

    It is suddenly obvious that Janet has *used the threat of abortion* (in other words, a willed refusal of regular patterns) to cause Tam Lin to reveal himself – but also that he has, in fact, been awaiting a maiden who will make the challenge, so that he may reveal the mode of his disenchantment.

9. Tam Lin reveals his true nature

Whereas in the version given above, Tam Lin 'falls from off his horse', other variants offer more revealing causes of his enchantment. He falls asleep under an apple tree, he passes through a magical chapel, or is overcome by sleep at a magical well. As a result of this he is captured by the Queen of Elfland. In other words, he passes into the under world while retaining his human origins. He makes the transition while in a sleep or trance, partly unwitting, without full command of his consciousness. His role of guardian fulfilling a stereotyped mode of magical behaviour, is the direct result of his automatic or unwilled enchantment. Until he is released from this first phase of his transmutation, he will act as phantom or guardian of the physical site to which he has become attuned.

The power of his release is 'true love', represented by fair Janet. The lack of distinction between her pregnancy and the manifestation of Tam Lin is significant in this context, for if she cannot redeem him in his original form, from the Otherworld, she will eventually bring him to birth after his entity has been broken down and destroyed (paid as a fine to Hell). The key concept here is *Man is Redeemed by Woman*, a concept which is repeated in the heretical Grail cycle.

As with Janet's challenge to gain Tam Lin's secret, her magical rescue is a willed alteration of the normal or expected pattern of events. In the first example, she turns against the laws of natural cause and effect in the outer world, by rejecting the so-called 'inevitable', the wheel of procreation. Her second challenge, however, is on an inner or magical level, whereby she moves against the current of the unseen powers, and seeks to suspend their cycle of operations also. She is stealing Tam Lin from the fairies – operating the magic known as 'the Path of the Thief'.

10. The nature of fairyland and the fine to Hell

Tam Lin's description of fairyland is heavily coloured by those of the Celtic Paradise. In many versions of the ballad, the pleasures of the Land are described, and one wonders why the hero might wish to leave!

'At the end of seven years/ They pay a fine to Hell.' Tam Lin is aware that his time in fairyland is limited – and the implications of this are far beyond the nursery level or guilt-ridden perversion of truth offered by a superficially Christian interpretation of the sequence.

It has been customary to rationalise the ballad by suggesting that the fairy folk stole Tam Lin to keep him as a sacrifice to the Devil, in order that their Paradisical state could be perpetuated.

Tam Lin is actually seeking a way free from the Wheel, on an inner or magical level. He acts as guardian of a power or sacred site (in this case linked to fertility), and despite the timeless and dreamlike quality of the state in which he finds himself, it is only a more subtle variant of the outer world.

At the end of a given period, he is offered up to the Powers of Destruction.

This is only normal. Every entity experiences this power of dissolution upon physical death.

In Tam Lin's case, he is singled out in a magical or *intermediate* role, so his cycle is not that of regular birth – life – death – rebirth. His entity, his self-awareness, is active in the Otherworld, through magical attunement to a function connected with the Land and fertility. He is honoured in this role by the beings that occupy the Otherworld, wherein his dual nature is given special consideration.

> 'I Tam-a-Line, on milk white steed,
> A gold star in my crown,
> Because I was an earthly knight
> They gave me this renown.'

As has been mentioned above, Tam Lin can only remain in his magical role for a certain period of time. At the end of that period he is offered up to Hell, or becomes subject to the powers of dissolution inherent in the underworld. Following this second death, he can only be reborn as a mortal child, and commence again upon the Wheel.

Once challenged, however, Tam Lin is able to reveal a way by which he might be liberated through transformation. As with other male characters in magic, he is incomplete without the female partner, and unable to transform without the vitalising fire of Janet's love.

11. The transformation at Hallow-e'en

The most obvious magical elements now begin to appear in the ballad. Janet must save her lover at Hallow-e'en – the festival which marks the ancient feast of the dead. At this time, the barriers between the outer and underworld were said to be weakened, and the dead could freely approach the living. Additionally, it was at this time that the Wild Hunt gathered in the souls of the dead – a period of transition. We can see from this significant use of Hallow-e'en a further reinforcement of the connection between 'fairy' lore and 'ancestor' lore.

Janet is told to hide at 'Miles Cross', which is sometimes seen as a suggestion of Christian power in her support. Crossroads, however, have an ancient significance, upon which Christianity merely added its own accumulation.

The Crossroads show *centrality within choice*. They are a place where the worlds meet, and the most deep and ancient gods are powers of the crossroads. Apart from the variants in which Janet questions her lover's origin in Christianity, 'Tam Lin' is a non-religious magical ballad. The action is completed by devotion and discipline, not by religious prayers or faith.

The fact that Tam Lin describes in advance the fairy court and the magical transformations is usually taken for granted, but indicates a typical magical operation. The guardian entities will not only effect magic, within the tradition, but they will also display, or inform the magician in advance, in an educative or helpful role. The simple acquisition of information, however, is not sufficient, for the sequences must be experienced.

In many versions of the ballad, the description is given, then repeated in its entirety during the chronological development of the disenchantment.

Three courts of Elfland are usually described – those that ride on black, brown and white horses. These correspond to three orders of inner-world beings in magic, and to three phases of changing matter in alchemy.

12. The transformations in effect

How do the transformations work? We are given a rationalised explanation on the superficial level of the ballad: the *fairies* change Tam Lin into shapes difficult for Janet to hold, so that they might keep him as their sacrifice to Hell.

There are obviously certain laws at work, as were observed in the earlier stages of the story where Tam Lin was summoned through the pulling of roses. It is clear that the fairies cannot act directly upon Janet; she is untouchable through her power of true love.

The ritualistic and game-playing aspects of traditional lore are extremely important, for they give considerable information regarding the laws that operate in magic, the inner worlds, and the human entity in its many interlinked aspects.

From the fairies' state of existence, Fair Janet is not only untouchable, she cannot be seen! Janet is the 'saving Grace', the secret spirit of redemption, and all changes, shapes and later curses are directed at, and through, Tam Lin.

We are following a description, in this ballad, of the interaction between a human being, certain underworld powers, and the mysterious spirit of origination and love. The interaction is catalytic, for until the element of 'grace' or 'redemption' enters the field of operation through love, Tam Lin cannot change. Once this new element is added, his startling transformations occur rapidly, and he is liberated as a new and reborn individual.

The strong links between this old Scottish ballad and the processes of alchemy should be obvious. Both describe a magical sequence of transmutations, effected by laws usually unperceived by mortal men, but nevertheless present and powerful in the heart of matter.

The actual sequence and presentation of the transformations varies considerably from text to text, but all involve the action of the Inner Fire, shape-changing, and purification through apparent destruction.

In his final incandescent transformation, as burning lead, Tam Lin is thrown into well-water (fire plunged into the water of earth) and becomes a naked knight. Janet wraps him in her green mantle, and he is transformed and returned to the Earth; she hides him from sight. His final transformation is a return.

13. The curses

For the first time, the Fairy Queen speaks out, and emits a sequence of curses. These prohibitions are suggestions of Tam Lin's new powers of perception as a transformed being, and are common to fairy and otherworld folklore. As Tam Lin has been saved from the underworld or fairyland, he can see into both realms, that of the human and of the non-human. Hence the threat that his eyes would have been plucked out, if only the Queen had known. A similar curse is made regarding his heart, the traditional centre of love. If he had had a heart of *stone*, he might never have been saved!

The malevolence of the Fairy Queen, in *Tam Lin* is rather different from her role in *Thomas the Rhymer*, but the information derived from both is, in fact, identical.

The comparison between the Queen in *Tam Lin*, and the Queen in *Thomas the Rhymer* reveals two basic aspects of the underworld. Briefly, the Queen in *Tam Lin* performs as a deeper level of guardian or controlling entity at the heart of the inner Mysteries of the underworld or Elfland. She is never approached direct, and no dialogue occurs with her. She is, in fact, operating in the role of an impersonal agency, fulfilling certain laws.

In *Thomas*, however, the Queen is directly concerned in an active dialogue with the hero, and becomes his redeemer through the offering of his love. In other words, the role of 'Queen' and 'Janet' are merged into one entity in the Thomas story, wherein she prohibits the hero from worshipping her as 'Queen of Heaven' – for she is *not* the Goddess.

In *Tam Lin*, the Queen, *not* activated or motivated by true love, can only be a deeper archetype. This concept is central to the practical operation of magic in the underworld, and should be fully understood before any experiments are attempted.

Indeed, the stories of Tam and Thomas should be seen as two operative variants of the same magical liberation process. In the first, the hero is saved by love from an exterior agency – either human love or divine grace – while in the second he is saved by that same divine power emanating from within himself.

For most of us, the first mode of liberation is the most likely, though the second is the true aim and function of the tradition. It would not be too daring to suggest that Tam Lin and Thomas may be taken sequentially for magical purposes.

The first ballad represents either a human male-female ritual operation and developed Mystery or the action of divine intervention through the cycles of the Wheel.

The second ballad represents this same use of polarities removed into an inner dimension, where the love-exchange occurs between the initiate and the inner world entity; through which love the divine redemption is activated.

The process described in Thomas, therefore, may be said to be a more advanced or developed means of achieving the liberation. Indeed, according to the laws of magic, Tam Lin, in his liberated form, has left a wrathful Fairy Queen behind in Elfland, and he is bound to reconcile and balance this state as his task in his new and innocent identity.

APPENDIX 4

Thomas Rhymer, a narrative magical ballad from Scottish tradition

Thomas Rhymer (Thomas of Ercledoune) was a thirteenth-century Scottish poet. This ballad, from oral collective tradition, remained in popular circulation until as late as the nineteenth century. Many of Thomas's vernacular *Prophecies* were published, and he is credited, perhaps doubtfully, with the first prose version of the story of *Tristan and Iseult*. The ballad represents a theme described by Kirk: the physical translation or transportation of a human into the fairy realm or underworld.

THOMAS THE RHYMER

A Scottish traditional ballad, based upon a historical person

Thomas the Rhymer, also known as Lord Learmont, Thomas of Ercledoune and 'True Thomas' lived during the thirteenth century. He is an extremely important person in the exposition of the hidden tradition, and forms one of a number of historical persons who may be termed Justified Men. These individuals are not necessarily connected in any fraternal manner, least of all by the spurious nonsense about 'secret orders' that has been forced into commercial popularity in recent years. They are connected through time, however, by a common thread of purpose and symbolic lore.

In magical terms, they are the prophets and teaching masters of the secret tradition, and may be said to exist metaphysically as a united body of consciousness which has expressed itself through specific members in serial time. Active magical groups who perpetuate genuine oral teaching traditions have various inner-world contacts whom they claim to be members of such a body. These are not, incidentally, mysterious immortals residing in seclusion in the Andes or on Mars, but are the conscious resonance or echo of certain advanced souls who are supposed to be concerned with the problems and spiritual development of those who are their children in outer time.

Whether or not one accepts this more recondite theory is a matter of indifference, for there are sufficient historical Justified Men within the narrow confines of British tradition, and they have left words, songs, poems and music behind, whereby those who follow in their footsteps through the underworld may be guided.

The list includes the Reverend Robert Kirk of Aberfoyle, Geoffrey of Monmouth, and the anonymous author of the Grail legends, while in more modern times we might include the authors George MacDonald and Charles Williams.

Not all metaphysicians or acclaimed philosophers or holy men belong to this grouping, for not all wisdom is gained through the underworld. The reader should be familiar by now with the hallmarks of the underworld tradition as suggested, and will be able to find clues in the works of great thinkers and metaphysicians. He or she will also be surprised at the absence of such clues in the works of apparently reputed representatives of Western religion, ethics and philosophy.

Thomas of Ercledoune, therefore, was renowned as a prophet during his own lifetime (and in his own country), and printed versions of his accurate predictions were circulated after his death, some still active as late as the nineteenth century. His pre-vision was the result of the underworld initiation, gained by his relationship with the Fairy Queen, as described in the famous old ballads and the Romance text which bear his name.

Thomas is also said to be the author of the earliest version of *Tristram and Iseult*, and may be rightly said to have had a far-reaching effect upon literature and upon the common imagination for the last 700 years. During the nineteenth century, his published prophecies caused Englishmen to flee to the hills in fear of an imminent disaster – which, unlike many of his quite accurate predictions, did not occur.

Living during the time of Robert the Bruce and William Wallace, with whom he was associated, Thomas is thought to have been a nationalist agent. This political role of the magus is found frequently throughout history. During Edward the First's bloody ravaging of Scotland, Thomas seems to have been an active traveller and seer in the nationalist cause.

Two traditions of his death are extant. The first is that he was murdered for political reasons by the followers of the Earl of March, and that he foresaw this death accurately. The second is that he lives on in the hollow Eildon hills of his home region in the Lowlands. Like Merlin, or Arthur, Thomas wears the mantle of the national hero who is also attuned to a deep and powerful myth; politics and magic are woven together in his cloak.

The large estates of Ercledoune were donated to the Church by Thomas's son, also called Thomas, thus fulfilling one prediction. The magical hawthorn tree of Thomas's initiation lived on until 1814, when it was blown down in a gale. The local people of Earlston on the River Leader, about thirty-five miles from Edinburgh, naturally attempted its revival by pouring whisky upon the roots, but to no avail. Thomas had prophesied that 'As long as the Thorn Tree stands,/ Ercledoune shall keep its lands.' In that same year, 600 years after these words were set down, a chain of financial disasters struck the community, and all common land was sold in payment of debts.

William Shakespeare was not only familiar with *The History of the Kings of Britain*, the magical history set out by Geoffrey of Monmouth, but also with the prophecies of Thomas the Rhymer. In a certain play, which it is traditionally unlucky to name, a clear adaptation of one of Thomas's verses is found. The original reads:

> Feddarate Castle sall ne'er be ta'en
> Till Fyvie wood to the seige is gaen.

Although these lines were adapted by Shakespeare to the castle of High Dunsinane, they were not proven true until a later century, when the troops of William of Orange made battering rams out of Fyvie wood, and entered the previously unconquered castle of Fedderate.

Like Merlin, or Nostradamus, or the Brahan Seer, Thomas has left a series of predictions as partial proof of the effectiveness of his initiation. As with many prophecies some are incomprehensible, others have been found accurate, but puerile demands of accuracy or vindication of the Otherworld powers overlook the essential importance of such individuals as Thomas.

They have left us clues, a method, a chart of rarely travelled realms. Do we dare to follow them, to try for ourselves what they have achieved? Or are we content to sit and quibble or merely read about the mighty men of old?

1. True Thomas lay o'er yon grassy bank
   And he beheld a lady gay,
   A lady that was both brisk and bold
   Come riding o'er the fernie brae.

2. Her skirt was of the grass-green silk,
   Her mantlet of the velvet fine,
   At ilka tett of her horses mane
   Hung fifty silver bells and nine.

3. True Thomas he took off his hat,
   And bowed him low down to his knee;
   'All hail thou mighty Queen of Heaven!
   For your peer on earth I ne'er did see!'

4. 'Oh no, oh no, True Thomas' she says,
   That name does not belong to me;
   I am but the Queen of Fair Elfland,
   That has come for to visit thee.

5. 'But ye maun go wi' me now Thomas,
   True Thomas ye maun go wi me,
   For ye maun serve me seven years
   Thro weel or wae as may change to be.'

6. She turned about her milk white steed,
   And took True Thomas up behind,
   And aye whene'er the bridle rang,
   The steed flew swifter than the wind.

7. For forty days and forty nights
   He wade thro red blude to the knee,
   And he saw neither sun nor moon,
   But heard the roaring of the sea.

8. O they rade on and further on,
   Until they came to a garden tree;
   'Light down, light down, ye ladie free,
   And I'll pull of that fruit for thee.'

9.   'O no, O no, True Thomas,' she says
      'That fruit maun not be touched by thee,
      For all the plagues that are in hell,
      Light on the fruit of this countrie.

10. 'But I have a loaf here in my lap,
      Likewise a bottle of red wine,
      And now ere we go further on,
      We'll rest awhile, and ye may dine.'

11. When he had eaten and drunk his fill,
      She said 'Lay your head upon my knee,
      And ere we climb yon high high hill,
      I will show you fairlies three.

12. 'Ah see ye not that broad broad road
      Tha lies by the lily leven?
      O that is the way of wickedness,
      Tho some call it the road to Heaven.

13. 'And see ye not that narrow narrow road,
      All beset with thorns and briers?
      O that is the way of righteousness,
      Tho after it but few enquires.

14. 'And see ye not that bonny bonny road,
      Which winds about the ferny brae?
      O that is the road to fair Elfland,
      Where you and I this night maun gae.

15. 'But Thomas you must hold your tongue,
      Whatever you may hear or see,
      For if one word you should chance to speak,
      You will never get back to your ain countrie.'

16. He has gotten a coat of the green green cloth,
      Likewise shoes of the velvet sheen,
      And till seven years were past and gone,
      True Thomas ne'er on earth was seen.

THOMAS THE RHYMER

Whereas many of the magical ballads consist of action, or action combined with visionary sequences, the traditional variants of Thomas the Rhymer are constructed from a series of interrelated visions, which are part of one united vision and initiation sequence. As this is one of the major keys to the underworld journey, it is worthy of careful examination and explanation, and will repay continued meditation and application. A long and complex Romance text exists, in which many of the specific elements of garden, fruit, Otherworld and related symbols are amplified in a conventional manner, but we will deal only with variants found in an oral tradition.

The plot moves through seven specific stages:

1. the Vision of the Queen of Elfland;
2. the Journey through the UnderWorld;
3. the Vision of the Tree;
4. the Ritual of Bread and Wine;
5. the Vision of the Three Roads;
6. the Vow of Silence;
7. the Return to the upper earth.

In some variants the order of the stages is different, while others give descriptions of Elfland and connected material; but the sequence given above, taken from the traditional source ballad used as our main example, is the correct magical order of events.

The vision of the Queen of Elfland (verses 1–5)

The seer or dreamer lies upon a grassy bank, beneath a hawthorn tree. Local tradition offered a specific tree as that used by Thomas, and enough has been said regarding trees and tree magic to make his actions clear to the reader. The hawthorn tree, growing upon a grassy bank, is the tree of initiation or of commencement. It is the only one that may have both a physical and metaphysical nature to regular outward-seeking human perception. This is the tree which early legends described as being composed of living green leaves and of flames, divided vertically, as in the vision of the knight Peredur. A thorn tree acts as the magical agent of birth in the ballad *The Cruel Mother*, which is linked to the redemptive symbolism of *The Wife of Usher's Well* and *The Maid and the Palmer*. The other two trees lie deeper in the underworld, and are only perceived by altered vision and a change of the direction of attention.

We should not, however, expect the three trees to be rigidly defined and separated, and in some aspects of the tradition they are implicit rather than specifically described. As with most magical symbols, we may detect their presence by function in the absence of direct description or visual imagery.

The thorn tree is one of the triad of oak, ash, and thorn, the three sacred trees of oral tradition, to which other trees may be added from ancient lore. This triad, however, is of considerable importance in connection to the three underworld trees. Thorn is the tree at the gate between the worlds, with its associations with May ceremonies, ill luck if picked at the wrong time, combined beauty of blossom and pain of thorn. Hawthorn, incidentally, is also a fruitbearing tree, and at one time the fruit was eaten and preserved. Like the rose, it carries blossom, thorns and fruit (rosehips), showing in nature the three stages of transformation: promise, pain and fulfilment. In the ballad of *Tam Lin*, Fair Janet summons Tam from fairyland by pulling roses and breaking thorns. We may regard the hawthorn and the rose as symbolically identical, and may further equate them with the Crown of Thorns of the Crucifixion.

Oak is the tree of the guardian, and of the sacrificed ones. In traditional magical visions, the way to the underworld or to the Grail castle is often marked by a small oaken door with a symbol carved above it. In some versions of the vision, the orchard of paradise, or the apple tree upon the hill, is surrounded by a ring of oaks. Those who meet the male guardian may encounter him at an oak tree, while those who are blessed like Thomas of Ercledoune, are guided by the Queen of Elfland direct to the fruit.

Ash, traditionally used for thrones, spears and sea-going vessels, may be equated with the third underworld tree, that of mediation.

The entire subject of detailed tree symbolism represents a very wide and complex field, which is not directly relevant to the present study, but the serious student or enquirer should consider native tree lore in depth.

A detailed study of ancient or oral tree lore is not a prerequisite of operational magic, and once again we should stress that basic initiatory patterns from common consciousness are far more important than scholarly or poetical attributions of woodland.

Thomas of Ercledoune, meanwhile, sleeps under the hawthorn tree. He beholds a 'lady gay' riding towards him. She is dressed in green, riding upon a horse, and her bridle is hung with silver bells. She is a nature power, the Isis of the ancients. Thomas erroneously titles her as 'mighty Queen of Heaven', and she immediately corrects him.

This apparently trivial detail of flattery is a very significant magical clue, which reveals important laws and powers of operation. Firstly, the human magician or initiate, whether male or female, is apt to confuse innerworld powers readily. Most modern occultists are so shocked at actually contacting any being whatsoever, that they invariably confuse the communication out of sheer surprise at their own partial success. The ballad teaches us two important rules or laws: (1) Do not confuse the powers one with another; (2) The powers themselves will tell you who or what they are.

In the case of rule (1) a power or being will only react properly if properly addressed, if you know the name, and an incorrect understanding of an innerworld being leads to flawed responses and energies *within the initiate*. There is no question of beings 'compelled' to be 'beneficial' by use of their names; this is juvenile and ignorant drivel. The beings are true to their own nature, but our understanding and channelling of that nature operates utterly through our own consciousness and physical bodies.

If we apply a power wrongly (call it by the wrong name, worship it as God, use it for foolish ends), then a self-perpetuating distortion occurs within our own matrix of body/consciousness. The Queen that approaches Thomas is the Queen of Elfland, and she specifically tells him that she is not the Queen of Heaven.

She is, in fact, an underworld or under-earth power, who manifests in upper-nature as growth, shown by her green skirt; sexual power of the body, shown by the horse; and the act of summoning or banishing, shown by the silver bells. These bells, which we may equate with the ancient sistrum of the Mysteries, feature frequently in traditional lore, and are associated with motion, the wind, speed and arousal.

Rule (2) is initially common sense, for Otherworld beings are self-declared by their symbolic appearance. A tradition, however, will also give specific clues and rules, via the instructional tales, songs and dramas preserved in common consciousness. It is vitally important to avoid the pitfalls represented by the models of psychology and 'unified' symbology, wherein all aspects of dream or vision are stuffed into intellectually contrived moulds for preservation and future labelling. All symbolism is *not* related to each and every part of the psyche and the universe, and both the psychological-materialist model and the religious-unity model that are rife in our modern culture are capable of great damage through their vapid lack of direction.

It is correct to state that the various symbolic entities merge one into the other, but this occurs only through transformation within the apprehending consciousness. In other words, we have to change before the links between the various keys and gates become active. In magical work, each innerworld being should be dealt with according to its own true appearance and nature, and the powers of one realm or World should not be forced through the matrices of another. As we shall soon discover, the Queen of Elfland may become the Queen of Heaven, but she is not so to our limited perceptions.

Thomas is obliged to go with the Queen – he has summoned her up from below, and has learnt her true name and nature. In some versions of the story, they embrace beneath the tree. The seer has aroused the inner power, and it carries him away. That this power is explicitly linked with sexual arousal is no mere coincidence, but an applied use of the inner life energies for specific ends.

Thomas is bound to the Queen for seven years (a period that appears in the ballads frequently in connection with vows, and applies to the old custom of 'trial' marriages derived from pre-Christian cultural patterns based upon inner or magical laws). We find this pattern repeated in the ballad of Lord Bateman, which represents a similar pattern of operation.

Thomas mounts upon the milk white steed, and they ride off together, 'and aye whene'er the bridle rang/The steed flew swifter than the wind.'

This concludes the first stage of the visionary sequence, and leads into:

The journey through the underworld (verses 6–8)

The magical steed is directed into the underworld, where neither sun nor moon are seen. The aroused power is directed downwards, and the imaginative ability of the seer or initiate perceives (a) a river of blood, and (b) a roaring sea. He is not, remember, wandering loosely in this potent realm, but is under the guidance of the Queen of Elfland, with whom he has exchanged vows.

We shall find the river of blood and the roaring sea again in another context, but they represent the individual's own bloodstream and flow of consciousness, perceived and experienced for the first time as identical with the greater blood and waters of created nature.

This experience or mode lasts forty days and nights for Thomas, and they emerge on the other side and ride further, until they come to 'a garden tree'. Any reasonably competent meditator will be able to confirm the *sound* of the roaring sea for his or herself, as this is a definite and commonly experienced inner sound that arises during certain stages of meditation. Deeper aspects of the sea and the blood are reached through the underworld journey, and are not usually accessible by regular or popularised meditational methods.

The vision of the tree (verses 8–9)

Thomas and the Queen of Elfland now arrive at the second tree. They have passed beneath, waded the river of blood, heard the roaring of the sea, and then have ridden *further on* to the apple or fruit tree that stands in the centre of the underworld. It is the tree of transformation, as Thomas is soon to discover.

The fruit is usually the apple, or in some versions it is a tree of mixed fruits, as in the ancient Irish legends. We now come to the true order of the giving and taking of fruits, which is well known to be corrupted in the orthodox Christian variants of the garden myth.

Thomas sees the fruit in its pure or unadapted state, as it grows at the heart of the underworld. He is comprehending the energies and the powers that hold creation together, and has travelled directly to this stage upon the magical horse, guided by his partner the Queen of Elfland. As he has not met the guardian, or been imprisoned, or exchanged riddles, or done battle, we may assume that this visionary sequence is the guiding pattern for the individual who has already undergone these processes.

If, for example, Thomas were to pluck the fruit and try to eat it, the guardian would be summoned. But he understands the true nature of his adventure, and offers to pluck the fruit as a gift to the Queen of Elfland. It is this act of simple sacrifice and direction that enables Thomas to continue his journey unchallenged, and furthermore, it is his offering of the fruit that transforms both himself *and the Queen.*

Ritual of bread and wine (verses 10–11)

She advises him not to touch the fruit, for it holds all the plagues of Hell. In its raw state, the fruit is poison. This advice is similar or parallel to an earlier admonition (omitted in our present text) that the river of blood is made of all the blood shed in the human world.

The Queen has a loaf of bread and a bottle of red wine, however, which she offers to Thomas. This is her response, her return of offered gifts, and they are the fruit transformed. In the Christian mass, as in the pagan, the bread is the body, and wine the blood. Both are transformed from the primal fruit.

If Thomas had eaten of the raw fruit, he would have been poisoned, and it is for this reason that the guardian is placed at the approach to the tree. Once past the guardian, the fruit has to be offered to the Queen, who now may transform the fruit into bread and wine, and herself into a deeper manifestation of divine power.

It is incorrect to assume that this symbolic sequence shows a crude 'Christianising' of a pagan Paradise myth. The sequence is exact and precise, and the difference between the pagan and Christian aspects of the Mystery are intimately linked to the 'Harrowing of Hell' by Christ, which enables the human initiate to pass to and fro in his name.

Once Thomas has partaken of the transformed fruit, given to him by the Queen, he has actually *replaced* the fruit upon the tree – by consuming it, by absorbing it into his own entity. This is such a significant action, that it demands further attention.

Thomas may not pluck the fruit, for it absorbs all the plagues of Hell, or all the sorrows of man and woman (in some versions). He offers to pluck it for the Queen of Elfland, and she responds by offering him bread and wine. If we filled out this section of the vision in detail, we might see that (a) Thomas does not actually pluck the fruit; he is willing to make that sacrifice without any conditions, but he is not required to do so. The implication is that this magical action is a lesser part, on the behalf of any individual, of some greater or spiritual sacrifice.

Thomas may reach the tree of transformation, but when he does so, the poisoned fruit is a deeper aspect of his own aroused fire, the power that has brought him through the underworld. He sees it as part of and in union with the normally modified powers of creation that are expressed in *form* in the outer or upper world. He is now confronted with *force*, the powers behind the form, and must therefore attune or offer these to their correct place and mode of operation. This is the Queen of Elfland.

We could say that at this stage (b) the fruit disappears from the tree, as a result of his offer of selflessness. It appears in the lap of the Queen, as bread and red wine, which she offers to him, with the suggestion that he may rest at this stage of the journey. The greater journey has not finished yet, but the traveller may rest and partake of the elements of the ritual of transformation beneath the tree.

When Thomas eats and drinks, he *re-transforms* the elements by their absorption within his entity. This is stage (c) of the central process, for at this stage, the fruit reappears upon the tree. Thomas has effectively changed the fruit, for it *reappears in a different place upon the tree.*

The entire sequence is one of polarity and catalysation, and must be considered carefully and meditatively to reveal its fullest insights.

The vision of the three roads (verses 11–14)

Once Thomas has taken the elements of bread and wine, he rests with his head upon the knee or lap of the Queen of Elfland. He is joined to her in trust, and this parallels the sexual implication of their vows and embraces in earlier verses and variants, although by this stage the concept of physical gratification has been transformed into an exchange of gifts and a shared journey and vision.

She shows him 'fairlies three', a vision within a vision, and the last stage of the journey. He would not be able to perceive this stage, let alone undertake to travel upon it, if he had not undergone the rituals of transformation at the second tree.

Once again, we should emphasise that the vision of the three roads is ancient and potent, and is not to be regarded as a mere orthodox gloss upon a pagan original. Even at this last stage of the journey, the initiate is offered a choice of how he or she may use the transformed power. The three choices are:

1. The Broad Road of wickedness that some say leads to Heaven;
2. The Narrow Road of righteousness, beset with thorns and briars;
3. The Bonny or Middle Road, to Elfland.

The first road is that of power expressed within the outer world, that of dominion, and the illusion of worldly hierarchies that impose order in the name of heaven. It represents not only the individual propensity for simple 'wickedness' but more esoterically the law that causes materially expressed hierarchies of spiritual or magical power to degenerate and become corrupt.

The adept is able to walk this road, either for personal ends or for time-bound hierarchical schemes of order and mass control. In either case they may seem to be the road to heaven, but terminate in evil.

The second road is that of individual sacrifice for specific aims. It represents the magical sacrifices of the ancient sacred kings, and the Sacrifice of Christ, which was a similar act upon a greater scale with far-reaching implications that are still developing in outer serial time. It may indeed be 'personal righteousness', but there is no moral issue at stake, for it is the ancient sacrificial way of containment and restriction of life-power for specific ends.

This road also is available to the adept, but the implications of the 'Harrowing of Hell' are that the third road is now open to any that are able to perceive it.

The third road, 'to fair Elfland', is the middle of the three roads. In the detailed vision, it may lead to the secret castle that houses the Grail, or to a low hill on which the third tree grows. This is the tree of mediation, the transmuted Grail, the power of the underworld transformed through human consciousness to encompass all worlds. It is to this place, upon the third road, that Thomas and the Fairy Queen 'this night maun gae'.

The vow of Silence (verse 15)

Thomas is advised not to speak while in fairyland, no matter what wonders are shown to him. This motif occurs in the Grail legends also, where it is tied to the asking of significant questions, a process usually associated with the confrontation of the guardian. In a deeper understanding of this admonition at the final stage of the journey, we may find some significant magical laws.

If Thomas speaks a word, he will not get back to his own country. This popular concept, which includes not only asking questions but eating of Otherworld food, and consorting with Otherworld lovers, both of which Thomas has already done, masks a magical law. As we are regarding the journey as a visionary and powerful transforming sequence, we now encounter the last choice upon the way.

Thomas may speak and question the wonders that he perceives, but by doing so, he commits himself forever to the Otherworld. He becomes, in modern terminology, an inner plane adept. He chooses to explore and grow within the inner realms, and not to return to the outer world. This is one of the choices offered to the initiate after physical death, and as we are considering the most recondite levels of the Mystery, we should consider this warning from the Queen of Elfland in such a light. Should Thomas direct his attentions towards further Mysteries, he will take the fourth road, which is unseen on the other side of the hill.

If he does not do so, he is able to return by the middle way to the outerworld, where he appears transformed by his experience.

The three roads may also be considered in the context of post-mortem metaphysics. The discarnate soul usually takes the 'broad broad way', in company with millions of others, following certain natural laws of attraction which are attuned by specific religions and mysteries, national group-souls, deep long-term aims of potent groups and patterns. These in turn are loosely related to certain stellar influences, and to the overall luminous attraction of Lucifer within the earth's planetary body. The broad way leads to rebirth.

The road of thorns and briars represents a voluntary incarnation in service of some higher aim or order – one who need not return to the planet or group worlds by impulse or attraction, but who chooses to do so out of love for those who suffer.

The middle way does not lead to incarnation from the inner to outer worlds, under normal circumstances. It may be specifically opened for communication and exchange 'across time', as we have seen in the summoning of the ancestors, and this is the simplest human level of its so-called discarnate operation. If the reader has followed the theory of the underworld initiation carefully, it will be clear that the usual concepts of life/death are irrelevant in such a context.

In a second level or mode, the middle way is available for exchange of energies between beings in different worlds. Spiritual enlightenment flows along this way, as do many of the concerted group rituals that involve beings of more than one realm or world operating together.

The third and most significant level of the middle way is the approach of the Saviour or Messiah. It is along this way that a divine one is born into the outer world, hence the conceptual structure of the Virgin Birth. This process, however, is merely a human reflection by divine power, of the descent into Hell, which is also a death/birth on the part of the Son of Light. The descent into Hell is synonymous and simultaneous with the conception, birth, sacrifice, death and resurrection. They only appear to be separated to the awareness locked into the illusion of serial time.

The return to upper earth (verse 16)

These are the choices, then, that Thomas has taken. He has emulated Christ in his descent into Hell, but has no personal motive therein. He chooses not to pass on to the unknown, but to return to the human group-world, where he acts as a prophet and as an example to all who may follow.

He is clothed in green, which signifies his union with the Land, a union that occurred as a direct result of his transformation within the underworld. His prophetic ability arises as a result of his mediating power, and not through the communication of 'familiar spirits'. He is able to perceive the apparent future, because it has already happened in the underworld.

The importance of Thomas, and of other historical persons who undertook the Journey is not merely poetical or inspirational. They still exist, they may still be contacted, and they are present in the inner worlds as teachers and guides.

APPENDIX 5

Prayers, Spells, and Charms from twentieth-century Devon and nineteenth-century Scotland

These examples come from a very large number of such prayers and healing charms preserved in British and Irish oral tradition. The Devon charms were noted by the Reverend Sabine Baring-Gould, and published in 1910. The Scottish invocations were current in oral tradition and noted in several variants by a number of collectors and scholars from the seventeenth to the nineteenth and twentieth centuries.

DEVONSHIRE FOLKLORE

For Burns or Scalds – Recite over the place:

> There were three Angels who came from the North,
> One bringing Fire, the other brought Frost,
> The other he was the Holy Ghost.
>> In Frost, out Fire! In the Name, etc.

For a Sprain – Recite: 'As Christ was riding over Crolly Bridge, His horse slid and sprained his leg. He alighted and spake the words: Bone to bone, and sinew to sinew! and blessed it and it became well, and so shall . . . become well. In the Name, etc.' Repeat thrice.
For Stanching Blood – Recite: 'Jesus was born in Bethlehem, baptised in the river of Jordan. The water was wide and the river was rude against the Holy Child. And He smote it with a rod, and it stood still, and so shall your blood stand still. In the Name, etc.' Repeat thrice.

Cure for Toothache – 'As our Blessed Lord and Saviour Jesus Christ were walking in the garden of Jerusalem, Jesus said unto Peter, Why weepest thou? Peter answered and said, Lord, I be terrible tormented with the toothache. Jesus said unto Peter, If thou wilt believe in Me and My words abide in thee, thou shall never more fill [*sic*] the pain in thy tooth. Peter cried out with tears, Lord, I believe, help thou my onbelieve [*sic*].'

Marianne had the gift of stanching blood even at a distance. On one occasion when hay was being cut, a man wounded himself at Kelly, some eight miles distant, and the blood flowed in streams. At once the farmer bade a man take a kerchief dipped in his blood and gallop as hard as he could to the tumble-down cottage, and get Marianne to bless the blood. He did so, and was gone some three hours. As soon as the old woman had charmed the kerchief the blood ceased to flow.

At one time, now thirty to forty years ago, it was not by any means uncommon for one to meet the village postman walking with one hand extended holding a kerchief that was sent to the White Witch to be blessed. The rag must touch no other human being till it reached her. Moreover, at my own village inn, people from a distance frequently lodged so as to be able to consult the White Witch, and my tenant, the landlady of the inn, was absolutely convinced of the efficacy of the cures wrought.

THE INVOCATION OF THE GRACES

Traditional invocation widespread in the Highlands and Islands of Scotland

> I bathe thy palms in showers of wine,
> In the lustral fire, in the seven elements,
> In the juice of rasps, in the milk of honey:
> And I place the nine pure choice graces
> In the fair fond face:
> The grace of form, the grace of voice,
> The grace of fortune, the grace of goodness,
> The grace of wisdom, the grace of charity,
> The grace of choice maidenliness,
> The grace of whole-souled loveliness,
> The grace of goodly speech.

Dark is yonder town, dark are those therein,
Thou art the white swan, going in among them,
Their hearts are under thy control
Their tongues are beneath thy sole,
Nor will they ever utter word to give thee offence.

Thine is the skill of the fairy woman
Thine is the virtue of Bride the calm,
Thine is the grace of Mary the mild,
Thine is the tact of the woman of Greece,
Thine is the beauty of Emir the lovely,
Thine is the tenderness of Darthula delightful,
Thine is the courage of Maebh the strong,
Thine is the charm of Binne-Bheul.

Thou art the door of the chief of hospitality,
Thou art the surpassing star of guidance
Thou art the step of the deer upon the hill,
Thou are the step of the steed upon the plain
Thou art the grace of the swan swimming,
Thou art the loveliness of all lovely desires.

Peter has come and Paul has come
James has come and John has come,
Muriel and Mary Virgin have come,
Uriel the all-beneficient has come,
Ariel the beauteousness of the young has come,
Gabriel the seer of the virgin has come
Raphael the prince of the valiant has come
Michael the chief of the hosts has come;
The spirit of true guidance has come,
And the king of kings has come upon the helm,
All to bestow on thee their affection and their love.

INVOCATION FOR JUSTICE

Traditional to the Scottish Highlands

Go at Dawn to a place where three streams meet. When the Sun rises
to the very top of the Hills, cup your hands and fill them with water

from the point where the streams meet. Dip your face into your hands full of the water, and repeat the invocation:

> I will wash my face in the nine rays of the sun
> As Mary washed her child in the rich fermented milk.
>
> Black is yonder town, black are those within,
> I am the white swan, queen above them all.
>
> I will travel in the name of God,
> In likeness of deer,
> In likeness of horse,
> In likeness of serpent,
> In likeness of king:
> Stronger will it be with me
> Than with all persons.

THE AUGURY OF MARY

This traditional augury from the Highlands of Scotland is said to have been employed by Mary to seek out the young Jesus when he was missing; he was in the Temple.

> God over me
> God before me
> God behind me,
> I on thy path oh God,
> Thou oh God
> In my steps.
>
> The augury made of Mary to her son
> The offering made of Bride through her palm.
> Sawest thou it, o king of life?
> Said the king of life that he saw.
>
> Son of beauteous Mary
> King of life,
> Give thou me eyes to see all my quest
> With grace that shall never fail
> Before me,
> That shall never quench or dim.

The augury made by Mary for her own offspring
When he was for a space missing . . .
Knowledge of truth,
Not knowledge of falsehood,
That I shall truly see all my quest.

Son of beauteous Mary
King of life,
Give thou my eyes to see all my quest
With grace that shall never fail, before me,
That shall never quench or dim.

APPENDIX 6

Brigit, the Fire Goddess

A short summary of the attributes and origins of Saint Brigit or Bride/Brigit, the Celtic goddess of fire, smithcraft, poetic inspiration, and healing.

Although Kirk does not mention Brigit by name, her traditions were deep-rooted and widespread in the Highlands and Islands, with many ceremonies attached to her worship. Many of the fundamental aspects of *The Secret Commonwealth*, such as eternal lamps, higher octaves of light and vision, magical or spiritual healing, are inherent to the cult of the goddess Brigit or the Saint Brigit.

Brigit (Brig, Briid, Bride or Brid) was the great Celtic goddess of fire and of fertility. She is still the guardian of the hearth in the Gaelic home, and when the fire is 'covered' for the night, so that the 'seed' of the fire may stay in the peat till the morning, a prayer is sometimes even now addressed to her. But her famous fire, tended by nineteen maidens, was at Kildare. An Archbishop of Dublin in the thirteenth century made an abortive attempt to suppress Brid's sacred fire – an indication that the fire was heathen and not Christian in origin.

Indeed, Brid's day, 1 February, was the date of one of the great pagan fire festivals. But Brid was not only a fire-goddess, she was also a goddess of fertility. Martin Martin in 1675 describes the following ceremony connected with Brid's day, observed in his time in the Western Islands of Scotland.

The mistress and servants of each family take a sheaf of oats and dress it up in women's apparel, put it in a large basket and lay a wooden club beside it, and this they call Briid's bed; and then the mistress and servants cry three times, 'Briid is come,' 'Briid is welcome.' This they do just before going to bed, and when they rise in the morning they look among the ashes, expecting to see the impression of Briid's club there; if they do, they reckon it a presage of a good crop and prosperous year, and the contrary they take as an ill omen.

The discerning reader will see indications of phallism in this strange ceremony, and so we find Brid as the aid-woman who assisted the expectant mother, and the bed incident just narrated was apparently converted into the legend that Brid aided the Virgin in her labours by making a bed for her.

Moore says that Brid or Bride was remembered in the Isle of Man in the eighteenth century, especially on 1 February, when housewives invited Bride into their homes, repeating in Manx: 'Bride, Bride, come to my house, come to my house to-night; open the door to Bride, and let Bride come in.'

Sir David Lindsay mentions an image of 'Sanct Bryde, weill carvit with ane kow,' and St Bride's Well in Kildrummy, Aberdeenshire, was famous for curing diseases in cattle: indeed, St Bride is thought by some to have displaced an older milking goddess.

The Brigantes, a people of North England, probably had Bride or Brig as their tutelary deity, and inscriptions found in Britain reading DEO SANCTO BERGANT ..., BRIGANTIA, NYMPHA BRIGANTIA, and BRIGANTIA SACRUM point to the cult of this famous goddess.

Brid was undoubtedly the greatest goddess of the Celts. Too powerful to be deposed, the Church had to make the best of things and converted her into a saint, sometimes called St Bride, sometimes even St Brigit or Bridget. Now St Bridget was probably a real personage, but the Christian Bridget has absorbed so much of the pagan Bride that some competent authorities have seriously doubted her existence. One example must suffice. The Celtic rite of dedication of a church was different from the Roman rite of Appellation, and required the presence of the founder on the spot. As Miss Arnold-Forster observes: 'St Bridget never crossed the Irish Channel, yet England can show some twenty dedications in her honour,' and we would add the fact that Wales can show about eighteen more. A real puzzle to the saint-lorist or hagiologist, but to us no puzzle at all. It is reasonable to suppose that there were once in Britain pagan temples erected in honour of the goddess Brid, and St Bridget is merely a Christian substitution for the pagan Brid –

an example of the way in which a Christian saint sometimes absorbs some of the things really belonging to a pagan deity.

APPENDIX 7

The *Vita Merlini* Cosmology

A central aspect of the twelfth-century biography of Merlin, formalised from Welsh bardic tradition by Geoffrey of Monmouth, this cosmology is very close indeed to that described by Kirk. Many aspects of the *Vita Merlini* correspond to beliefs reported in *The Secret Commonwealth* as being active in seventeenth-century Gaelic tradition. Both the twelfth-century Merlin texts and perennial oral tradition are rooted in Celtic pagan religion.

CREATION OF THE WORLD

ELEMENTS AND CIRCLES

Meanwhile Taliesin had come to see Merlin the prophet who had sent for him to find out what caused wind or rainstorms, for both together were drawing near and the clouds were thickening. He drew the following illustrations under the guidance of Minerva his associate.

'Out of nothing the Creator of the world produced *four elements* that they might be the prior cause as well as the material for creating all things when they were joined together in harmony: the *heaven* which He adorned with *stars* and which stands on high and embraces everything like the shells surrounding a nut; then He made the *air*, fit for forming sounds, through the medium of which day and night present the stars; the *sea* which girds the land in four circles, and with its mighty refluence so strikes the air as to generate the *winds* which are said to be four in number; as a foundation He placed the earth, standing by its own strength and not lightly moved, which is divided into five parts, whereof the middle one is not habitable because of the heat and the two furthest are shunned because of their cold. To the last two He gave a moderate temperature and these are inhabited by *men* and *birds* and herds of *wild beasts*.

CLOUDS, RAIN, WINDS

He added clouds to the sky so that they might furnish sudden showers to make the fruits of the trees and of the ground grow with their gentle sprinkling. With the help of the sun these are filled like water skins from the rivers by a hidden law, and then, rising through the upper air, they pour out the water they have taken up, driven by the force of the winds. From them come rainstorms, snow, and round hail when the cold damp wind breathes out its blasts which, penetrating the clouds, drive out the streams just as they make them. Each of the winds takes to itself a nature of its own from its proximity to the zone where it is born.

ORDERS OF SPIRITS

Beyond the firmament in which He fixed the shining stars He placed the *ethereal heaven* and gave it as a habitation to troops of *angels* whom the worthy contemplation and marvellous sweetness of God refresh throughout the ages. This also He adorned with stars and the *shining sun*, laying down the law, by which a star should run within fixed limits through the part of heaven entrusted to it.

He afterwards placed beneath this the *airy heavens*, shining with the lunary body, which throughout their high places abound in troops of *spirits* who sympathise or rejoice with us as things go well or ill. They are accustomed to carry the prayers of men through the air and to beseech God to have mercy on them, and to bring back intimations of God's will, either in dreams or by voice or by other signs, through doing which they become wise.

The space below the moon abounds in evil *demons*, who are skilled to cheat and deceive and tempt us; often they assume a body made of air and appear to us and many things often follow. They even hold intercourse with women and make them pregnant, generating in an unholy manner. So therefore He made the heavens to be inhabited by *three orders of spirits* that each one might look out for something and renew the world from the renewed seed of things.

THE SEA

The sea too He distinguished by various forms that from itself it might produce the forms of things, generating throughout the ages. Indeed, part of it burns and part freezes and the third part, getting a moderate temperature from the other two, ministers to our needs.

That part which burns surrounds a gulf and fierce people, and its divers streams, flowing back, separate this from the orb of earth, increasing fire from fire. Thither descend those who transgress the laws and reject God; whither their perverse will leads them they go, eager to destroy what is forbidden to them. There stands the stern-eyed judge holding his equal balance and giving to each one his merits and his deserts.

The second part, which freezes, rolls about the foreshorn sands which it is the first to generate from the near-by vapour when it is mingled with the rays of Venus's star. This star, the Arabs say, makes shining gems when it passes through the Fishes while its waters look back at the flames. These gems by their virtues benefit the people who wear them, and make many well and keep them so. These too the Maker distinguished by their kinds as He did all things, that we might discern from their forms and from their colours of what kinds they are and of what manifest virtues.

The third form of the sea which circles our orb furnishes us many good things owing to its proximity. For it nourishes fishes and produces salt in abundance, and bears back and forth ships carrying our commerce, by the profits of which the poor man becomes suddenly rich. It makes fertile the neighbouring soil and feeds the birds who, they say, are generated from it along with the fishes and, although unlike, are moved by the laws of nature. The sea is dominated by them more than by the fishes, and they fly lightly up from it through space and seek the lofty regions. But its moisture drives the fishes beneath the waves and keeps them there, and does not permit them to live when they get out into the dry light. These too the Maker distinguished according to their species and to the different ones gave each his nature, whence through the ages they were to become admirable and healthful to the sick.

FISH

For men say that the *barbel* restrains the heat of passion but makes blind those who eat it often. The *thymallus*, which has its name from the flower thyme, smells so that it betrays the fish that often eat of it until all the fishes in the river smell like itself. They say that the *muraenas*, contrary to all laws, are all the feminine sex, yet they copulate and reproduce and multiply their offspring from a different kind of seed. For often snakes come together along the shore where they are, and they make the sound of pleasing hissing and, calling out the muraenas, join with them according to custom. It is also remarkable that the *remora*, half a foot long, holds fast the ship to which it adheres at sea just as though it were fast aground, and does not permit the vessel to move until it lets go; because of this power it is to be feared. And that which they call the *swordfish*, because it does injury with its sharp beak, people often fear to approach with a ship when it is swimming, for if it is captured it at once makes a hole in the vessel, cuts it in pieces, and sinks it suddenly in a whirlpool. The *serra* makes itself feared by ships because of its crest; it fixes to them as it swims underneath, cuts them to pieces and throws the pieces into the waves, wherefore its crest is to be feared like a sword. And the *water dragon*, which men say has poison under its wings, is to be feared by those who capture it; whenever it strikes it does harm by pouring out its poison. The *torpedo* is said to have another kind of destruction, for if any one touches it when it is alive, straightway his arms and his feet grow torpid and so do his other members and they lose their functions just as though they were dead, so harmful is the emanation of its body.

APPENDIX 8

Robert Kirk's Glossary

As written by Kirk at the conclusion of *The Secret Commonwealth*.

ROBERT KIRK'S GLOSSARY

An Exposition of the difficult Words in the foregoing Treatises.

A

Amphibious	he that liveth as well on Water, as on Land
Amulet	a preservative against inchantment, bewitching or poisons, to be hanged about the neck
Addle	rotten or spilt
Astral Body	An Artificial Body assum'd by any spirit
Antidot	A counter-poyson, or a medicine against poyson
Atomes	Motes in the Sun, or a thing so smal it cannot be divided
Antipodes	people which go directly against us, with the soles of their feet against ours
Abstruse	hid, or shut up close
Aer	one of the four Elements, the aire which liveth, or is in the aire
Adapted	being made very fit
ascititious	chosen admitted associate or strange

B

Bier	a coffin that is always reserv'd for the corps of the poor people, and keept within the church
Badgers	Broks
Boaz	in strength, meaning the powers thereof shall continue

C

Compact	appointment or confederacie
Candidats	they y^t stand & labour for any offic cloathed in white robs because among the Romans they used white robs, a suiter or he that endeavoureth to obtaine any thing
Convictions	assurances
circumference	compass
centre	the poynt in the midst of any round thing, the centre of a Circle
Colonies	Inhabitants sent to a forrein countrey
Collegue	a fellow companion or co-partner in office
Coalesce	to grow together or to increase
Chimaeras	a feign'd Beast
comment	exposition
Chameleon	a litl beast that doth easyly change itselfe into all colours, and is nourished only with the air
Cockatrice	a serpent killing man and beast with his breath and sight
condensed	made thick or hard

D

defaecat	uncorrupt, pure and clean from dreggs
Delphian	two faced, ambiguous and doubtful
disquisition	tryal of a thing
Deception	beguiling
drein	dry up
cogniscance	examination determination or tryal by a judge

E

Elves	a Tribe of the Fayries that use not to exceed an ell in stature
Exuviae	a cast skine of an Snake or adder
Entities	Beings
Exorcism	conjuration
Æther	the firmament, skye, light, brightness
Eccho	a sound rebounding to a noise or voice in a valley or wood, a resounding or giving again of the voice
Element	the fundation of anything, the first principal cause of instruction, whereof / all things take their beginning, being, four, Fire, Air, Water, Earth

F

Faunes	a Rank of daemons betwixt Angels and men
Fanaticism	fanatic = mad and foolish
facultie	Virtue or strength in a thing, a power to do or speak

G

Gradation	a form of speaking when the sentence goes by degrees or steps going up in order one after another

H

Heterogeneus	of another kind
Helix	a kind of Ivie, bearing no berries, running round
Hypochondriak Melancholly	a windie melancholly which is bred of ach and sorness about the short ribs from whence a black flemme arysing doth hurt and trouble the mind
Heluo	He that in eating and drinking destroyeth his substance as gluttons Wasters & prodigals

I

Intrigues	politicks secrets or mysteries
Immersed	plunged drenched or dipt in water
Iachin	he will establish his promise toward his house
Impetus	violence vehemencie
Insects	any smal vermine divided in the body between the head and the belly, having no flesh, blood or sinew, such as flies, gnats, pismires or Emmets.
Intellectual	belonging to understanding

L

Lychnobious	he that instead of the day, useth the night, and liveth as it were by candle night
Legerdemain	sleight of hand
Legion	is a Brigad or Regiment of 6000 footmen and 732 horsmen

M

Magic	Witchcraft Sorcerie Soothsaying
Malefice	an ill, naughtie deed, and mischievous act
Mole	a moudewort
Mole	a litl brown spot in any part of mans body
Meridian	mid-day, or noontide

N

Necromancie	divination by calling on Spirits
Nymphs	Goddess of waters, maids or Brids
Noctambulo	he that riseth and walketh in the night tim, when asleep

O

optic	pertaining to sight. optici nervi. the sinews that bring the virtue of seeing into the eye

Oracle	a prophesie or prediction
obvious	gentle and easy, or that which meeteth with one
orb	a world, a Region, a countrey

P

puppet	a Babie or imag like a child
phantasms	Vain Visions, false imagination
phantastic	a foolish vain vision
paroxisms	a rage, a fit of distraction, or rush
plaginism	a stealing of men servants or children
parson	a curate, or paroch priest
parelij	two or thre suns appearing throw a refraction of a cloud
philtres	a love potion
paralell	such-like
python	a prophesieing spirit, or a man possesst with such a spirit, a Bellirummer as it were the ill spirit speaking out of his belly
phaenomenon	an appearance either in the heaven or in the air
propagated	to make to spread, or to multiply

Q

quaintly	neatly Eloquently

R

Rick	staks
Rosicrucian	a possessor of a magical-like art
Rabbinical	Jewish
Radicate	that hath taken root
Receptacle	a place to receive & keep things safe in, a place of confort or refuge

S

superterraneans	are wee that live on the surface of the Earth
subterraneans	those people y^t lives in the cavities of the Earth

Sith's	people at rest and in peac
Seer	wizard or a people of the second sight are they that telleth of things befor or to come after
Succint	short or brief
Struma	Kings-Evil
Suanoch	mantle or cloak
Shrug	to be aversed
Syrenes	sea monsters
Scrutiny	a diligent search

T

Terrestrial Bodie	is a body made of the four Elements
Thesi	a position, the natural primitive word qʳof other are derived and deduced, a termination
Transmigration	a departing from one place to dwel in another
Topical-spirits	that haunt one place and not another
Tendons	smal things lik hair hinging at the roots of trees, or a litle vein
tragical	cruel outragious

W

Utopias	a nation invented by mens fancy's
Vehicles	chariots, or a general name of all things serving to carry
Wight	a cunning man

X

Zijim jiim and Ochin	were aither wild Beasts or fowls or ostridges or spirits, qʳby Satan deluded man as by the fairies, goblins &c.

APPENDIX 9

Angels and Fairies

An extract from Harold Bailey's *Archaic England*. The connection between fairies, Otherworld lovers, *daemones*, and angels is found in *The Secret Commonwealth*. It also plays an important part in the Merlin tradition as reported by Geoffrey of Monmouth and other medieval chroniclers.

In Glamorganshire there is a village known as Angel Town, and Pembroke is Angle or Nangle: Adamnan, in his *Life of Columba*, records that the saint opened his books and 'read them on the Hill of the Angels, where once on a time the citizens of the Heavenly Country were seen to descend to hold conversation with the blessed man'. Upon this his editor comments: 'this is the knoll called "great fairies hill". Not far away is the "little fairies hill". The fairies hills of pagan mythology became angels hills in the minds of the early Christian saints.' One may be permitted to question whether this metamorphosis really occurred, and whether the idea of Angels or Angles is not actually older than even the Onslows or *ange* lows. The Irish trinity of St Patrick, St Bride, and St Columba, are said all to lie buried in one spot at Dunence, and the place-name *Dunence* seemingly implies that that site was an *on's low*, or *dun ange*. The term *angel* is now understood to mean radically a messenger, but the primary sense must have been deeper than this: in English *ingle* – as in ingle-nook – meant *fire*, and according to Skeat it also meant a darling or a paramour.

A SHORT BIBLIOGRAPHY

Many of the books listed contain extensive bibliographies for further reading and reference.

1   *The Secret Commonwealth*, edited by A. Lang, David Nutt, London, 1893.
2   *The Secret Commonwealth*, edited by S. Sanderson, Folklore Society, Cambridge, Mistletoe Series. Includes a detailed bibliography of manuscript sources and relevant printed reference works, plus a short biography of Robert Kirk, and a discussion of fairy tradition in folklore.
3   *Samuel Pepys: (Vol. 3) The Saviour of the Navy*, Arthur Bryant, Collins, London, 1938.
4   *John Dee*, Charlotte Fell Smith, Constable, London, 1909; *The Heptarchia Mystica of John Dee*, edited by Robert Turner, Hermetic Opus Sourceworks Series, no. 17, Edinburgh, 1983; 'John Dee, The Elizabethan Merlin', Gareth Knight in *Merlin and Woman*, edited by R. J. Stewart, Blandford Press, London, 1988.
5   *The Fairy Faith in Celtic Countries*, W.Y. Evans Wentz, Oxford University Press, 1911. New edition with Foreword by Kathleen Raine, Colin Smythe Ltd, Gerrards Cross, England/Humanities Press, Atlantic Highlands, New Jersey, USA, 1977. The scholarly and poetic background to this major work, researched and written during the 'Celtic revival' of the early twentieth century, is discussed by Dr Raine in her Foreword to the 1977 edition.
6   *The Folklore of the Scottish Highlands*, A. Ross, Batsford, London, 1976; also *Pagan Celtic Britain*, Cardinal, 1974.
7   *A Collection of Highland Rites and Customs*, edited by J. L. Campbell, Folklore Society, Cambridge, 1975; *A Description of the Western Islands of Scotland*, London, 1703, republished

Eneas Mackay, Stirling, 1934; *Deuteroscopia*, Rev. John Fraser, Symson, Edinburgh 1707; *A Journey to the Western Islands of Scotland*, Samuel Johnson, Strahan and Cadell, London, 1775; *Witchcraft and Second Sight in the Highlands and Islands of Scotland*, J.G.Campbell, Glasgow, 1902.

8   *Elements of Prophecy*, R.J. Stewart, Element Books, Shaftesbury, 1990.

9   *Carmina Gadelica*, edited by Alexander Carmichael, 6 Vols, Scottish Academic Press, Edinburgh, 1972

10   *The Presence of the Past*, R. Sheldrake, Collins, London, 1987.

11   *The Under World Initiation*, R.J. Stewart, Aquarian Press, Wellingborough, 1986, 1989.

12   *Celtic Gods and Goddesses*, R.J. Stewart, Blandford Press, London, 1990; *Elements of Creation Myth*, R.J. Stewart, Element Books, Shaftesbury, 1989; *Living Magical Arts*, R.J. Stewart, Blandford Press, Poole, 1987; *Advanced Magical Arts*, R. J. Stewart, Element Books, Shaftesbury, 1988.

13   *Celtic Heritage*, A. & B. Rees, Thames and Hudson, London, 1974.

14   Extensive notes and references to these studies are found in 13 above.

15   See *Elements of Creation Myth*, 12 above.

16   See 10 above and other books by R. Sheldrake.

17   *Legendary Britain*, John Matthews and R.J. Stewart, Blandford Press, London, 1989.

18   *The Mystic Life of Merlin*, R.J. Stewart, Penguin- Arkana, London 1986, 1988. Contains translation of the original text by Geoffrey of Monmouth, with a detailed commentary.

19   *The Waters of The Gap: The Roman Celtic mythology and magic of Aquae Sulis*, R.J. Stewart, Bath City Council, 1980. Reprinted with new Foreword, Arcania-Ashgrove Press, Bath, 1989.

20   *The Prophetic Vision of Merlin*, R.J. Stewart, Penguin-Arkana, London, 1986, 1988. Contains translation of the original text by Geoffrey of Monmouth, with a detailed commentary.

21   *The Rosicrucian Vault*, Caitlin Matthews, as an Appendix to 11 above.

22   'The Immortal Hour', Fiona Macleod (William Sharp) in vol. VII, *Collected Works*, Heinemann, London, 1933. *The Immortal Hour*, Opera by Rutland Boughton (with libretto), Hyperion Records, London (new digital recording, 1987).

23   *Where is St George?* R.J. Stewart, 1988, Blandford Press. See also 11 above.

24 See 8 above for a discussion of hepatoscopy, and the classical theory as described by Plato in the *Timaeus*.

25 *Sketches descriptive of Picturesque Scenery on the Southern Confines of Perthshire*, P. Graham, 1806, 1812.

26 See 5 above.

27 *Barbarossa, a short biography*, R.J. Stewart, Firebird Books, Poole, 1988.

28 See 2 and 9 above.

INDEX

Aberfoyle 71, 95, 107
Abraham 49
Adam 55, 61, 71
Adepts 116
AE, (George Russell) 2
Aeniad 103
Agrippa, Cornelius 50, 114
Alchemy 14, 109
Allies 5, 73, 115, 118
Amulets 66
Ancestors 12, 34, 56, 60, 73, 93, 97, 101
Animals 22, 23, 27, 30, 77, 83, 88, 96
Anointing 37
Apollo 91, 103
Apparitions 10, 32, 33, 44, 51, 109
Aquae-vita 30
Archangels 48, 75
Archons 75
Areopagita, Dionysus 114
Aristotle 44
Arrows 23, 43, 44
Atheism 10, 11, 92, 114
Augury 104

Balaam 34
Ballads, fairy lore in 6, 85, 99, 107
Balsam, healing 35, 53, 104
Barbados, seers deported to 45
Beasts, 29, 30, 51, 66, 88, 96
Bible, the 3, 26, 27, 63, 68, 91, 117
Birds 24, 30, 37, 51, 96, 116
Bladud, King 86
Blood 29, 54, 58, 85, 117
Bloodlines 104
Boaz 52
Boyle, Robert 3, 39, 89, 109
Brigid 85
Brownies 22, 52, 77, 117
Buddhism 93, 101

Celts 80, 87, 96
Children, fairy 23, 24, 25, 32, 36, 39, 57,
    60, 62, 84, 86, 95, 97, 98, 102, 104,
    106, 109, 120
Christening 107
Christianity 2, 7, 72, 75, 81, 89, 94, 97,
    106, 111

Churchyard 31, 68, 97
Clairvoyance 97
Commonwealth, the 1, 2, 3, 6, 8, 9, 10,
    11, 12, 13, 56, 72, 76
Communion 23, 112, 114, 116, 118
Compact, fairy 35, 46, 56, 64, 70, 120
Companion 24, 72, 73, 83, 96, 114, 121
Conjurer, seer described as 31
Convocations 26
Corpse 23, 33, 43, 82, 101
Cosmology 17, 73, 82, 87, 116
Counter-charm 25, 27, 91
Covenant 61, 111
Co-habitants 57
Co-walker 24, 46, 73, 77, 82, 83, 96, 99,
    114, 119
Creation 26, 55, 88

Daemon 54, 86
Daemones 18, 54, 72, 73, 75, 76, 99, 117
Darts, fairy 30
Death 3, 8, 25, 28, 33, 38, 40, 50, 58, 70,
    82, 87, 88, 94, 97
Death's-head 28
Death-dog 94
Death-messenger 28
Dee, Dr. John 4, 5
Deuteronomy 50, 63
Devil 34, 115
Devils 26, 49, 52, 59, 61, 68, 69, 72, 87
Divination 105
Divinities 77
Doomsday 22, 78, 80
Doppleganger 82
Double, astral or fairy 40, 82, 92
Double-man 23, 82
Dragon 48
Dreaming 46, 114

Ecclesiastes 54
Echo 11, 24, 46, 83
Eildon 108
Elements, the 18, 24, 70, 82, 83, 88, 91,
    97, 117
Elfland 6, 85, 86, 108, 111, 115
Elf-bolt 94
Elf-shot, 30

Elias 49
Elijah 33, 65
Elisha 33, 54, 60
Enchanters 25, 68
England 4, 51, 53, 91, 93, 94, 110, 116, 117
Enoch 71
Entities 4, 7, 47, 72, 73, 74, 76, 77, 80, 83, 88, 97, 103, 114, 119, 120
Eon 67, 70
Epiphanies 75
Equinox 78
Er 28
Essenes 35
Europe 4, 74, 92
Evil 3, 44, 47, 49, 50, 54, 58, 59, 60, 62, 63, 65, 68, 69, 70, 72, 73, 87, 91, 111, 112, 118, 120
Exodus 56
Exorcism 57, 69
Eye, powers of 3, 25, 37, 39, 46, 47, 48, 60, 68, 69, 86, 106, 109, 111, 112

Fairyland 37, 86, 107
Fairy-hill 31
Fairy-lore 18, 29
Fairy-tale 53
Fama Fraternitas, the 91
Fasting 37
Fauns 21
Festivals 80
Fey 29
Fire 25, 26, 42, 43, 53, 85
Flight 86
Flint, arrows made of 29, 52, 94
Folklore 1, 2, 3, 5, 8, 9, 13, 14, 16, 17, 73, 77, 84, 96, 101, 117
Folklorists 73, 76, 107
Forecasting 30, 96
Forefathers 61
Foreknowledge 96
Foreseeing 33
Foresight 35, 105

Gaels 8
Ghosts 31, 54, 55, 59, 73, 74
Giants 62, 64
Glastonbury 85, 108
God 25, 27, 55, 59, 60, 61, 67, 70, 91, 118
Goddess 8, 85, 86, 97
Goddesses 73, 75, 82, 85, 93
Gods 50, 53, 64, 65, 69, 73, 75, 77, 82, 93, 97

God-king 86, 108
Gospel, the 22, 76, 118
Greatrakes, Valentine 35
Guardian 23, 48, 49, 83, 108, 114
Guardianship 107

Hair-tedder 24
Halloween 80
Harp 27, 53
Haunting 24, 31, 60
Healers 13, 95
Healing 1, 9, 10, 12, 13, 66, 95, 104, 107, 118, 120
Health 29, 58, 70
Heart 64, 68, 115
Heaven 51, 68, 86, 93
Hebrews 54
Hecate 8
Helix 33, 100, 101
Hell 26, 51, 85, 89
Heresy 94, 119
Heron 24
Highlanders, Scottish 10, 12, 21, 23, 39, 50, 52, 55, 66, 109, 115
Highlands, Scottish 2, 26, 40, 41, 44, 50, 106, 111, 115
Hollow-cavern 51
Horsemen 41

Iachin 52
Iamblichus 74, 75
Idolatry 70
Images 7, 17, 46, 54, 70, 75, 92, 97, 118
Imagination 31, 46, 50, 74, 85, 119
Immanuel 67, 70
Incantations 13
Initiation 83, 100, 101, 102, 103
Inshalladine 71
Ireland 8, 26, 38, 75, 80, 81, 85
Irish, (Scots) 2, 17, 21, 28, 35, 66, 88, 96

Jesus 27, 34, 47, 49, 54, 55, 64, 67, 69, 85, 88, 89, 103, 117
Jews 59, 65
Job 54
Johnson, Dr 2, 102
Jude 71
Judgement 39, 44, 58, 63, 90, 98

Kabbalah 82, 93
Knothole 102

Lamps, fairy and otherworld 25, 37, 53, 84, 85, 92, 106, 108
Legend 14, 86, 88, 92, 96
Loadstone, power of 26, 60
Love 27, 40, 42, 65, 71
Lucifer 64
Luke 33, 54

Mabinogion, The 88, 96
Macrimmond 115
Magic 4, 6, 24, 84, 100, 119, 120
Manucodiata 51, 116
Mason Word, the 52, 117
Materialism 10, 11, 92, 114
Matthew 64, 103
Mcintyre 37
Medicine 4, 66
Mediumship 6
Melrose 108
Merlin 5, 32, 76, 86, 88, 99, 108, 109, 116
Metaphysics 4, 14, 44, 83, 103
Middle-Earth 23, 82
Minerva 85
Mirror 12, 25, 44, 46, 81, 83
Monmouth, Geoffrey of 5, 76, 86, 99, 110, 116
Monteith 71
Moon 53, 75, 85
Mortals 23, 26, 29, 32, 49, 52, 55, 86, 120
Moses 47, 49
Music 52, 93, 115
Mysticism 77, 83, 101
Myth 88, 89, 96, 99
Mythology 13, 77, 82, 117
Myths 14, 84, 88, 99

Naaman 33
Necromancy 8, 59, 63
Noctambulo 50, 115
Nostrademus 4, 5, 9, 74
Nurses, fairy tradition of 25, 85, 86, 87, 95, 106
Nymphs 32, 49

Ochim 55
Octave 9, 104, 114
Ointment 37, 46, 106
Orpheus 88
Otherworld 72, 84, 85, 86, 92, 99, 104, 111, 114, 120

Paganism 6, 10, 11, 22, 76, 99, 118, 120
Palsy 66, 69
Paradise 51, 116
Paramours, fairy 50
Phantasms 33
Phillipians 89
Philosophers 9, 49, 54, 117, 118
Philosophy 14, 77, 88, 96, 110
Philtres 65
Plato 9, 82, 114
Platonists 64
Poetry 6, 51, 85, 115
Poets 49, 114, 115
Polarity 77, 83, 120
Poltergeists 6
Power 1, 6, 9, 12, 27, 29, 37, 45, 52, 54, 55, 58, 64, 65, 70, 75, 84, 95, 97, 101, 107, 117, 118
Prayers 13, 63, 64, 85, 115
Predictions 39, 45, 47, 48, 109
Priestess 91, 103
Priests 108
Procreation 58, 119
Prognostication 23, 35, 43, 104
Prophecies 5, 85, 86, 109
Prophecy 3, 6, 103, 109
Prophets 33, 47, 59, 101, 108, 120
Purgatory 55
Pythagoras 49, 114
Pythoness 34, 91, 103

Quintessence 24, 57

Raptures 29, 48, 58, 95
Reflection 24, 25, 44, 46, 83
Regeneration 97
Reincarnation 81, 88, 94
Religion 10, 11, 27, 32, 62, 63, 73, 77, 78, 80, 87, 88, 89, 97, 99, 100, 105, 106, 114, 118, 121
Revelation 48, 54, 70, 99, 118
Rhymer, Thomas 6, 85, 108, 115
Ritual 83, 84, 97, 99, 100, 101, 105, 107
Rosicrucians the 91

Sabbaths 24
Sadducees 47
Saludadors 3
Samhain 80
Samuel 3, 54, 111
Satyrs 24, 53, 55
Saul 52
Saviour 54, 55, 64, 89

Science 9, 13, 35, 59, 77, 103, 117
Scott, Sir Walter 2, 111
Scripture 53, 54, 55, 60, 117, 119
Seer 1, 12, 23, 26, 27, 29, 30, 32, 33, 34,
    37, 38, 39, 41, 42, 43, 45, 46, 48, 58,
    60, 72, 82, 90, 95, 96, 100, 101, 102,
    103, 105, 106, 108, 109, 110, 111,
    112, 118, 119
Seership 4, 6, 7, 9, 10, 12, 14, 33, 89, 90,
    100, 103, 104, 105, 109, 118, 120
Shamanism 6, 101
Shape-changing 86
Shoulder-blade, divination by 35
Shrines 77
Shroud 30, 97
Simulacra 75
Sirens 32
Sleep-walkers 50
Smithcraft 85
Socrates 49, 114
Soul, the 31, 46, 57, 66, 94, 98, 118, 121
Sound 27, 29, 35, 54
Spectres 51
Spell 27, 67, 68, 69, 90, 115
Spells 4, 63, 64, 65, 66, 68, 95, 104, 115,
    118
Spirit 4, 13, 14, 15, 25, 27, 46, 49, 50,
    51, 52, 54, 57, 58, 65, 90, 91, 94,
    105, 107, 118, 119
Spirits 4, 12, 21, 24, 28, 30, 31, 34, 35, 47,
    48, 49, 50, 51, 52, 54, 55, 57, 58, 59,
    62, 63, 73, 75, 80, 82, 87, 93, 98, 104,
    106, 107, 111, 114, 115, 117, 118
Spiritualism 6, 7
Spring 32, 37, 78
Stars 47, 82, 85
Stillingfleet, Rev. 10
Story-telling 16
Stroking, therapeutic 35, 53, 104
Subterraneans 24, 26, 29, 32, 33, 54, 72,
    83, 95, 98
Succubi 32, 50, 62, 98
Supernatural 12, 38, 60, 74, 75, 90, 98,
    111
Supersition 5, 10, 37, 70, 106, 107, 116
Superterranean 10, 14, 23, 25, 56, 62, 82,
    118
Suspiria de Profundis 92
Synagogues 24
Syrians 33

Talismans 70
Tan Lin, the ballad of 99, 107

Tarbett, Lord 8, 45, 90, 109, 110, 111,
    120
Tedder, hair 33, 100, 101
Telepathy 5, 112
Temptation 16, 34, 103
Tradition 1, 2, 3, 5, 6, 7, 9, 12, 13, 14, 16,
    18, 52, 55, 64, 65, 69, 73, 74, 75, 76,
    77, 80, 81, 83, 84, 85, 88, 90, 93, 94,
    95, 96, 97, 98, 99, 106, 107, 114, 115,
    116, 117
Trinity, the 18, 60, 70, 97

Uist 40
Ullapool 41
Unbeast, the 67
Underground 6, 12, 57, 81, 92, 109
Underworld 6, 8, 12, 13, 77, 80, 82, 83,
    85, 87, 89, 92, 93, 95, 97, 101, 106,
    115, 116, 118

Virgil 103
Vision 30, 31, 32, 33, 34, 38, 40, 41, 43,
    44, 45, 47, 50, 51, 59, 60, 74, 85, 86,
    102, 104, 110
Visions 44, 48, 49, 58, 90, 103, 110, 111,
    114, 119
Void, the 22, 28, 62, 93, 94

Wasting-double 106
Watchers 48
Water 25, 46, 69, 85, 109
Wemyss 51
Wentz, Evans 2, 107
Werewolf 92
Wickedness 56, 86
Wind 25, 28, 33, 68, 94, 102
Winding-shroud 30
Winter 12, 37, 78, 101, 108
Witchcraft 11, 46, 56, 94, 105, 110, 118
Witches 24, 27, 46, 58, 63, 84, 92, 95,
    105
Worship 23, 97
Wounding 29, 50, 94, 117
Wounds, prevention and cure of 4, 26,
    29, 92, 94, 95
Wraith 28, 94

Yeats, W.B 2

Zacharias 33
Zijim-jiim 55

Lightning Source UK Ltd.
Milton Keynes UK
UKHW01f0035170718
325817UK00006B/340/P